KAM.

BEGINNERS

200+ Sex Positions for Couples with Detailed Practical Illustrations and Secret Tips for Men and Women to Fire Up Your Life. The Essential Guide to Enjoy Incredible Sex

Emily Lewis

Table of Contents

Introduction

When it is well practiced, the Kama Sutra is able to bring many health benefits to our physical, physiological and mental well being. There are different reasons behind this, some of which include the yoga basis to the sexual positions, tantric massage, as well as encouraging closer relationships between couples.

There are many benefits to the yoga positioning in the lovemaking aspect to the Kama Sutra. Yoga is well known to provide many benefits from flexibility and relaxation to increased blood flow and mental clarity.

Tantric massage is an erotic massage that encourages partners to really get to know others bodies. By becoming familiar with each other's bodies, partners are able to learn what their partner finds arousing outside of the typical arousal spots.

The encouragement of healthy relationships between partners occurs both in and out of the bedroom. The Kama Sutra recognizes that there is a connection between the intimate parts of a relationship as well as the everyday motions a couple goes through. Being able to connect in and outside of the bedroom helps a couple to establish a nurturing bond that cannot be broken.

There are many other ways that a healthy sex life, as laid out in the Kama Sutra, can contribute to your health and happiness.

When they are done correctly, the Kama Sutra positions are designed to encourage bonding and curiosity between partners. Some of the more advanced positions also foster trust in one another in order to balance and not be hurt. Learning how to pleasure one another is a journey that is exciting and invigorating and allows for new feelings to emerge in the relationship.

Sex also aids in the production of hormones such as oxytocin, which keeps you healthy and glowing. Engaging in one hour of sexual activity is equivalent to fifteen minutes of jogging, and can burn up to two hundred calories per session. Sex is thought to fight stress, increase heart health and those who engage in regular sex are said to be less impacted by arthritis, depression, anxiety, and stress.

This isn't to say that you can go and have sex with anyone in order to reap the benefits of having sex. The Kama Sutra promoted having intimate sex with one partner. In order to have intimate sex, there needs to be a connection on a level deeper than simply physical. The needs to be a mental, emotional and spiritual connection between two partners in order to really get any of the benefits of having sex in the way the Kama Sutra lays out.

Today there are many people who feel as though their sex life has fallen into a rut. The act of making love becomes boring and tedious and couples tend to get lost in the day to day routine of their lives. This was true back in the ancient Indian times as well as today. This was why the Kama Sutra spent a lot of time discussing foreplay.

When a relationship fails to have a healthy sex life, the couple often finds that they will eventually have problems in other aspects of their relationship. The act of making love creates a closeness between a man and woman, and this is what the Kama Sutra was created to cultivate.

Chapter 1. Sexual Compatibility

What is Sexual Compatibility?

One of the most powerful features of a good relationship is sexual compatibility. At first, you could assume it is all about how much you and your partner want the same things in bed. Possibly, how your partner has body features like tits, backsides, dick or straight shoulders the way you have always wanted. This is not completely off the mark, but sexual compatibility goes way beyond such thinking.

Imagine a relationship where your partner has the exact things you want. The height, the eyeballs, the body fitness and the smile you always adore, but you cannot understand each other. You cannot tell if they are having a good or bad time. She doesn't know when to let things go with you. He couldn't tell when you are angry, tired, happy or feigning your emotions too, do you think you could be a good fit for such a person? Do you think you would relish having sex with him? It is applicable to both men and women. Sometimes, he wants to talk and not have sex, but you have no idea and you pressed for it. You both had sex, but it definitely won't be one she enjoyed.

Women put on a show sometimes. A woman would frown and scream about everything in the house as if she hated you. But all she wants is you. She wants you to drag her into your arms and kiss her. She wants to melt in your arms and passionately make love with you. If you are sexually compatible, you would fully understand her when she falls into a mood like this, and you know exactly what to do. But if you are not sexually compatible, you might flare up at her weird behaviors. Label her all sorts and storm out of the house in anger.

Men have their styles of attracting you without saying a word too. Each person has a different style of communicating with their partner and they frantically hope you could understand without waiting for them to explain in words.

Unquestionably, sexual compatibility goes beyond having the same taste in bed. These additional factors can determine how you well you would get along in the bedroom and beyond. So, you should recognize them all so you can tell whether if you are compatible with your partner or not yet.

Why It Is Important?

- To know if you both have the same urge for sex. Your partner has to have the same definition of sex as you. For instance, 'do I consider anal, oral and so on as sex?' Whatever your answer is, she should have the same answers too. 'Do I feel a mad drive for sex at least 5 times in a week?' 'Can I go up to 5 rounds each time I have sex?' 'Is there a sex style, sex position that is so heavenly to me, and does my partner enjoy exploring that same style?' You can begin to relax if your partner has the same answer to these questions, your compatibility level is gaining some scale.

6

- You know exactly what turns her on. If you and your partner can read each other, you edge closer to sexual compatibility than you can imagine. You can tell when your partner is turned on and all they need is a powerful fuck till they reach orgasm. You can also tell when you should just give a cuddle and ignore your sexual drive. Your partner can tell the same about you too. You both possess the trick to get your partner up and very hard, you also know things that would instantly turn your partner off. Having this ability is crucial to your sexual compatibility with your partner.

- Sex environment. Quite strange but certainly true. We all love to have sex in different conditions. Do you enjoy having sex in a completely dark place? Do you prefer a mildly lit or a very bright room? Or are you the type who loved getting laid in quick silent places and not even rooms? Is your partner the same? Some people love a man who could slide into the kitchen quietly and turn them off while quinoa or steaks are still on fire. They loved having sex in a quick spot like that, the bathroom, the walkway, the table and not just the bedroom. You need to find out the position of sex that thrills you more, and then analyze how much your spouse dazzle at such sex styles. It is completely 'okay' to prefer having sex in a bedroom, as long as it is how your partners loves it too. With this your sexual compatibility is certain.

- How much of affection can you both displays outside? No hard feelings, but some persons would not even want to hold your hand

7

in public. It is not to say they cannot take your breath away in the bedroom, but public display isn't just for them. If you are the contrary type, the person who loves to cuddle, hug, and even kiss in public, you might have a rough time getting along with a partner who doesn't fancy that, and it might affect your bedroom relationship. It doesn't get any better when you are both out in a garden or a cinema and you found couples doing exactly what your partner won't.

- Technology in Sex. Quite awkward, but it is another factor to consider. Your wife or husband might be electrified by the thoughts of recording your sex now and then. He might want you to share nudes, flirt on texts et cetera. Your love life would get a zillion times easier if you are the same type too. But if not, it's a complete breakdown that can lead you to marriage blank.

Chapter 2. Learning to Make Love

Things to Know for Your First Time

Foreplay is probably the most important aspect of making love with someone. It makes you feel more connected to your partner and it also ensures that you are as aroused as possible when the act of intercourse finally happens. During foreplay, blood rushes to the genital region of both the man and the woman and creates sensitivity and lubrication. This is a major contributor to the intensity of the orgasm a person is going to experience during intercourse. When both partners aren't at their peak arousal when intercourse takes place, it can leave the partner who wasn't as aroused disappointed. As intercourse begins, like foreplay, it encourages the blood to rush to the genitals, and it can take longer for intercourse to bring satisfaction. The following preparations are sure to increase your excitement and pleasure and will be more than worth the effort:

- The most important thing to do before being intimate with your partner is to take the time to relax the body and mind from an exhausting day at work. You can do this in whatever way is best for you, whether it's a hot shower, a run, or a nap. This is going to ensure that you aren't going to be distracted thinking about your day at work while you are spending time with your partner. The act of lovemaking is a connection between two bodies that exchange their positive energies to heal and relieve the other from a hectic life.

- The Kama Sutra states that upon entering the pleasure room, both partners would cleanse themselves. Ensuring you are clean is important to make sure that your body is appealing to your partner. Many people today still like to be clean, and like their partners to be clean, before pursuing intimate activities. This is also a great opportunity for you to cleanse your day away and start your time with your partner in a fresh frame of mind. Cleansing your body gives your partner an opportunity to explore more intimate areas of your body bringing a lot of pleasure to you.

- In love-making, smelling fresh plays a vital role. Though fragrance enters your body from the nose, it directly has an effect on your brain which further boosts your mood and escalates your pulse. Wear a perfume that is going to arouse your partner's senses. Choosing a scent that they like is preferable to choosing one that you like, as one that you like may not be arousing to them. For example, if you like the scent of vanilla but your partner finds it off-putting, it could potentially ruin your intimacy. If you aren't sure what scents your partner likes, it is advised that you either wear a neutral scent or no scent at all.

- Another suggestion is to wear something that is going to be visually pleasing to your partner. This doesn't mean that it has to be a revealing piece of lingerie, it can be a color your partner likes, or even a particular outfit your partner often compliments.

- The Kama Sutra encourages embracing your partner before making love, but this isn't referring to an everyday hug. When you embrace the way the Kama Sutra instructs, you are using much more than just your arms. You are going to touch, rub, and press with the front part of your body. This creates a touching sensation all over the body. Moving your cheeks, nose and lips simultaneously while hugging your partner can stimulate your and their senses.

- Make the bed with clean sheets and pillowcases. Place one pillow at each end of the bed. Beside the bed, have a couch and a low table or stool that you can place your massage oils, strawberries, or any other items you may choose to use during your love-making. Tip: Adding furry or soft feathers or similar articles that could be ticklish to your love-making scene can awaken your sense of touch.

- Enjoy a light meal together. Avoid heavy and greasy foods, as these will make you feel uncomfortable and even sleepy after eating. Instead, feed each other small bites of fruits or aphrodisiac foods that you both enjoy. It is said that a man can be fed pineapple juice for a sweeter ejaculation.

- While you are eating, start a romantic conversation. Show your partner how much you love them, trust them, and care about them. Appreciating each other can boost confidence and ease partners of anxiety and nervousness.

- **Aphrodisiac Foods:** An aphrodisiac is something that stimulates sexual desire. There are some foods that are believed to stimulate pleasure centers and increase the sex drive and desire of the people eating them. In the Kama Sutra, the aphrodisiac foods that were recommended included rice mixed with wild honey. Another recommendation of the Kama Sutra was a mixture of ground up pumpkin seeds, almonds, sugar cane root, and strips of bamboo that were mixed with milk and honey.

Best Love Making Position

1. Wide Open Position

The woman is lying down on her back. Lowers down her upper half of the body and raises back her hips. The entrance of the vagina is stretched wide.

Tips: A pillow should place under her back.

2. Crossed Legs

The woman lies down with her buttocks near the edge of the bed. The male kneels or stands on the other side, entering her from the front. However, the legs do not sit astride the male hips but are raised upwards and crossed together. The male holds them up for balance as he penetrates her in this position. He can also choose to cross and uncross her legs for additional stimulation. For the most part however, the legs remain crossed, keeping the vagina pleasantly tight for the male.

Tips: The position of the legs makes it impossible to stimulate the clitoris.

Benefits: This also leaves the female free to play with her breasts.

3. Crab posture

Crab posture (Karkata) is a complex position.

The woman unites with her man by keeping one of her legs above head and the other is stretched out, and then holds the later up, and then stretch the other and continues to do so alternatively.

Tips: This position should not be used during rough sex because it can damage the penis.

Benefits: It will be great deal of penile flexibility because she will be bending the penis back quite a bit when she sits on him

4. The Lazy Man

The man is lying with his legs dangling at the edges of the bed and his feet on the ground while the woman, resting on him, keeps her thighs wide apart to allow the partner to stimulate her clitoris and she to caress the base of the penis.

Tips: To increase penetration, she moves rhythmically, gripping her knees.

Benefits: This position offers man a particularly exciting view of his partner's penetration, buttocks and sex. Taking advantage of the free hands, it can also stimulate the anal area and the buttocks.

5. The Eight

The woman is lying on her back, with her legs slightly open, possibly with a pillow under her back to facilitate penetration. The man is lying on the woman, and has his hands on one side and the other of her head, with his arms stretched out as if doing the push-ups.

Tips: The woman holds her hands on the man's hips, and helps him forms "8" numbers with the hips while he is inside her.

Benefits: The 8 "relaxed" is the symbol of infinity, and it seems like a good promise to be made in two!

6. Penetrating the Eye

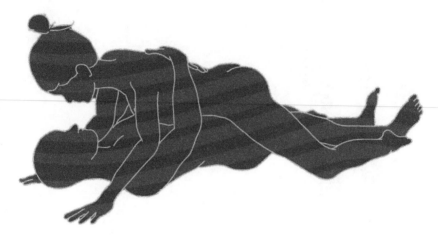

The female starts by kneeling on the bed and spreading her thighs wide open. The male also kneels and enters her from behind, plastering his upper body to her back and kissing the nape of her neck with each thrust.

Tips: It's also a fairly easy position and best done in front of the mirror, allowing both male and female added stimulation during sex.

Benefits: In this position, both the male and female are free to play with different erogenous zones such as the ass of the male, the clitoris, the breast, the lips, the nape, the U-Zone and more.

7. Bandoleer

The woman is lying on her back with her legs raised and her knees joined against her chest; the man kneels and penetrates her.

Benefits: In this position, the G-spot is stimulated more intensely.

8. Utphallaka

The man kneels on the bed. The woman lies down on her back, raises her buttocks and wraps her legs around him. As the man penetrates her, the woman arches her back, getting help from him, who holds her hands under her back.

9. Reverse Cowgirl

This is the position where the man lies down and the woman sit in the cow style but reversed in a way that her hip touches the man's pelvis area. The man penetrates from down and the woman does the up and down movement and not the man.

Tips: The man can support the woman by holding her hip and supporting the movement by giving his strength.

10. Deep Dish

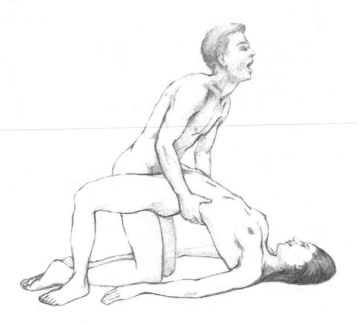

The woman lies down with her legs apart and the man sits with his knee down and holding the woman's legs and the hips area of the woman will be on the thigh of the man. The man will do all the up and down movements and then woman can put pressure lying down.

Tips: It can make variations by moving the women in a sitting position from the earlier position, then the woman can do all the movements and the male partner can give her support by holding her.

Benefits: The position wills make the intercourse deeper.

Chapter 3. Sex Positions for Beginners

11. The Missionary Position

This is perhaps the most widely known and used sexual position in the world. It is also deemed as the most conservative as this act can be done with very little effort (and can also be done without disrupting the sheets too much).

The man and the woman perform this act in horizontal to one another

Tips: there is little to no chance of seeing any other body parts unless the man sits u.

Benefits: This position allows eye and body contact which makes it favoured by both males and females.

24

12. The Yawning Position

The woman lies on her back and stretches her legs up and outward until they are totally extended and widespread in the air. The man kneels and enters the woman while holding the woman's hands for support.

Tips: The legs can be raised to the armpits of the man.

Benefits: This position is a great position for beginners, as it is simple and easily varied to find the perfect angle for each partner.

13. The Close-Up

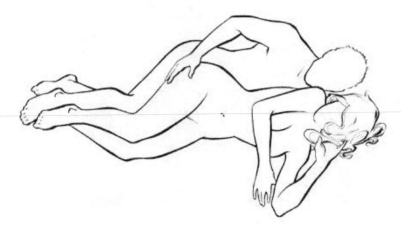

The woman lies on her side on the bed while the man snuggles in behind her. The woman can feel him right up against her back.

The woman then spreads her legs and helps the man enter. He then draws his legs together and begins to thrust. At the same time, the woman closes her legs, holding him inside her.

Tips: This position is intended for snuggling.

Benefits: It is a very intimate position that allows for feeling your partners body all over in skin-to-skin intimacy.

14. The Rocking Horse

The man begins by sitting cross-legged on the bed. He supports himself with his arms behind him resting on the bed. The woman then kneels on him and spreads her legs on either side of his pelvis, slowly lowering herself onto him. The woman then holds the man close with their bodies touching. She will move up and down using her thigh muscles and a circular motion of her hips.

Tips: Although this position will put you and your partner into an unfamiliar pose, it is not a difficult pose to achieve.

Benefits: It allows for increased pleasure for both the man and the woman

15. The Cross

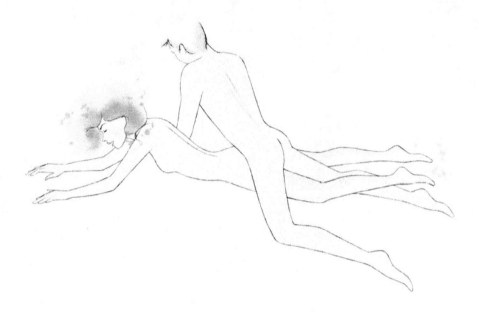

The woman lies on her back with one leg extended and one leg bent while the man holds the bent leg. The man rests on his knees and places his thigh over the woman's extended leg. The woman then takes her bent leg and touches the backside of it to the chest of the man, with her leg straight up against the man.

Benefits: Another variation of the missionary position, this position ensures deep penetrative lovemaking and gives the woman a higher level of stimulation.

16. The Prone Tiger

The man sits on the bed or another hard surface with his legs outstretched. The woman straddles his body with her back to his front. She lowers herself onto his lingam from the straddling position. Once the man has penetrated the woman, she stretches her legs out as straight as possible and grabs onto the man's feet for leverage.

Benefits: This is a fun position for couples to try if they are looking for something a little different to try.

17. The Magic Mountain

Make a mountain out of firm pillows. You want the mountain to be high enough so that when the woman is on her knees and leans over, her hips are at a right angle. After the woman leans against the pillows, the man kneels behind her with his legs on the outside of hers. From this position he penetrates her.

Tips: This position is a rear-entry position that doesn't require the woman to hold her weight up.

Benefits: The positions above are all relatively easy to achieve, although they may take some practice to get perfect. Each one of them is going to bring your lovemaking to a higher level than ever before. Not all of the above positions may be right for you and your partner, however, experimenting with them is half the fun. Once you have had fun with the above poses, if you are feeling more adventurous, read on to find some more challenging poses you and your partner can experiment with while love-making.

18. Short Stack Sally

This is a lying down with woman on top which guys love. However, there is a twist to this one. The female is turned around facing away from you looking up at the ceiling.

You enter her from the back, takes a little teamwork here and you help her slide and not bounce. Very effectual and saves her the bouncing. The old bouncing and sitting up straddles and facing away would have the male sliding out and coitus interrupts would happen ad nauseam.

Tips: If you are a bit weighty as a woman that's great because curves and voluptuousness is sexy, but you have to make sex comfortable for you too and not just your partner.

Benefits: This one is not as hard as it seems. This in highly effectual and puts a smile on your face pronto

19. Saint

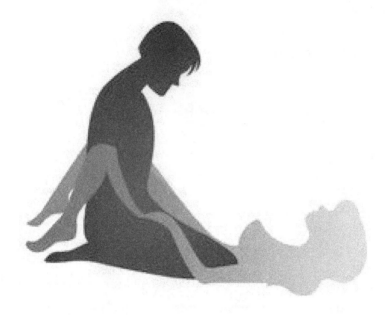

The standard variation of this family has the man sitting while kneeling backward and the woman lying with her back on the floor and lower part of her body lying on his lap with knees folded upward. This position allows access to both holes together with the intent of going slower or a bit harsher according to the choice of both partners. **Tips:** Both partners are face-to-face, providing enough opportunity for kissing, licking or boobs sucking, together with the option of body licking for the woman too. The woman on her knees mat fastens the mobility. Otherwise, the speedy penetration isn't guaranteed. But the thing that is ensured is a deeper penetration with strong clitoral stimulation together with intense rubbing when going curvy inside the vaginal or anal hole. Moving on while rotating the hips, also helped by the man with his hands on her hips, could make the sex more enjoyable and enthusiastic. Mildness comes naturally by going harsh.

Benefits: This is one of the favorable positions of kneeling family as it offers an explorative approach towards the holes together with fishy movements.

20. Kneeling Saint

Woman with folded knees sits on his lap while hugging him deeply and kissing him with her full. On the other hand, the man with folded knees sits on the floor while making room for her on his lap and hugging her intensely, kissing her face and sucking her boobs with his full. This position, with enough kissing and hugging experiences, becomes favorite and enjoyable for many people who love to indulge deeply into sex.

Tips: Another fiesta is the position of the vagina that lies right in front of the man's penis, allowing frictionless inclusion with curvy angles. These penetration angles happen with more rubbing, stimulating wild sex and allow to go deep inside the vaginal hole. The anal inclusion isn't guaranteed a bit deep as the anal hole isn't as near as the vaginal hole. But the anal gaping, together with friction to the walls of anus, might turn both partners into wild beasts by going harsher and slightly slap on her ass.

Benefits: This is quite an amazing sex position as it offers more divine and enthusiastic sex giving intense hugging experiences.

21. Pressed Guard

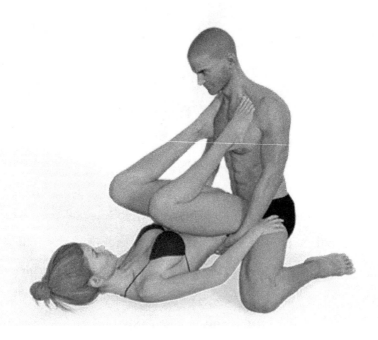

Another folded knees sex position from the family of kneeling sex positions is pressed guard.

In this position, the woman presses her knees on the man's chest and allows him the frictionless access to her holes by putting both the holes right in front of the man's penis. The woman lies on the floor with her back while the man sits on his knees and lifts her ass by putting his hands beneath her ass. This lets him go deep and straight into her vaginal and anal hole as both the holes allow their access.

Tips: The better options could be to explore the holes and enjoy the feelings by tilting, changing angles and letting the partner take over.

Benefits: Normally, this position involves deeper penetration with a harsher approach, but the woman can control the inclusion by pressing on his chest if she feels pain due to the harsh approach.

22. Bent Guard

This is quite similar to the previous sex position as it also involves the woman lying on the floor with her back and ass up in her partner's lap and feet on his chest by bending the knees, allowing him to stay in control and have fun with her holes. On the other hand, the man is sitting on his knees while leaning a bit forward and allowing her eye contact. Man can go deep with harsh intent and use force to tighten her legs and feel the heat of the moment.

Tips: He can also raise the sensation and joys by slapping her a bit on her ass, with her accordance. The woman could feel every inch of his penis when included in the anal hole with the use of force and rubbing her gaping. More friction involves when the penis goes in the vagina, resulting in a strong stimulation and greater orgasms for her.

Benefits: This position involves better angles and better sex with easy penis inclusion into the vagina and anal hole. The experience of sex would be quite sensational and fantastic with higher satisfaction up to offloading for both partners.

23. Folded Guard

Another interesting position in the family of kneeling sex positions. It allows the woman to lie on the floor with her shoulders and her pelvis lifted by the man with his hands beneath her buttocks and her legs up in the air, hanging on his shoulders. The woman being lifted off the ground and her holes right in front of his penis invite his penis to go deep and mobilize her body by doing fast in and out from the vagina or anal hole. Anal sex could be a lot sensational and enthusiastic as the anal hole allows straight inclusion and turns the sex into a mild experience. While going into the vagina could be a curvy inclusion as pussy lies a bit higher than the penis, guaranteeing more rubbing and more gentle experience by using slight force, pushing her forward by the man.

Tips: This position could be tried with some tilt and angles to get the most out of it.

Benefits: This position offers greater mobility with a large area of skin touching each other and making physical contact sensational by praising the partner.

24. Bent Candle

The bent candle is another sex position in the family of kneeling sex positions. This position is known all over the world, and very appreciated by couples. In this position, the woman lies on the ground with her back touching the ground and her legs up in the air, hanging straight up with the body of her partner. On the other hand, the man is standing on her knees with his legs folded and hands on the knees of his female partner, holding her tightly to support her legs and making room for his penis in her pelvis. The woman is lying straight on the ground with face and boobs up, encouraging him to kiss and fuck thoroughly.

Tips: The man could go gently and slower, if he wants, to feel the sensations and satisfy his partner by offloading her from cum. whereas, he may go hard to feel the heat of the moment.

Benefits: The sex would be quite reluctant and sensational as it offers deep penetration with straight and curvy inclusion inside the vaginal and anal hole, allowing both partners to move fast or slow according to their choice.

25. Folded Candle

The folded candle is much similar to the bent candle. It also offers the woman lying with a straight back on the ground and her legs straighten up in the air, touching the body of the man and giving him enormous exposure of her holes together with the option of choosing any of the holes to go deep. Her legs are slightly folded and leaned forward towards her abdomen. While the man, behind her pelvis, is standing on kneeling knees and holding her buttocks and thighs with his hands to pull her towards himself to guarantee deep penetration.

Benefits: This position allows him to expose both of the holes and go deep in the vaginal hole as the vagina is pretty much right in front of his penis and waiting for the shattering by a cock. The anal hole is a bit beneath the penis as her pelvis is lifted by the man above the ground. Therefore, it favours the anal gaping and makes it sensational, together with strong clitoral stimulation by rubbing of the penis with the inner lips of the vagina.

26. Tilted Candle

Another enthusiastic position in the family of kneeling sex positions is the tilted candle. In this position, the woman lies on the ground with her shoulders and head rested on the ground. While his lower part is lifted above the ground by the man with his hands beneath her buttocks, the woman places both of her legs on the same side of the man, leaving her a bit imbalanced.

Tips: The best approach to enjoy this position is to raise her pelvis up and tilt her lower body to make room for the penis and exposure. Trying all angles of this position can offer to explore the beauties of sex either going gentle or harsh, relying on mutual understanding.

Benefits: This position offers the man a lot more creativity to fasten his strokes as he has more room for his penis to strike hard to reach the depths of the vagina. In this way, he can make sex really hard for the woman and make him immediately offloading with cum and satisfying her completely.

27. Split Kneeling

The position is quite similar for both partners. The woman is standing on a knee, touching the ground while another crossing with a knee of the man. The male partner is also standing in an identical situation. This position offers both partners the sensations of the sex on knees while holding each other tightly. The man holds her buttocks to push her forward and hug her tightly to ingest her boobs in his chest and feel the heat of the moment. The female partner hugs him tightly with her hands around his neck and rests her head on his shoulder.

Tips: To go deep inside the anal hole, he must lift her a bit to make penis inclusion possible. Going inside the anal hole could be a lot difficult but quite amazing and sensational due to its enjoyment factor.

Benefits: The man can go forward with powerful strikes to hit deep inside her vaginal hole and to ensure strong clitoral stimulation.

28. The Lateral Join

The woman starts with her back to her partner and lies down on her side. The man kneels behind the woman so that the two bodies are perpendicular. The man takes the woman's lower leg and moves it, while penetrating her. She takes her upper leg and stretches it slightly to give him better visibility. To get used to the push he can hold the woman by the hips.

29. The Gold Triangle

At first glance, the position of the Golden Triangle recalls the classic missionary position: the woman lying down with the man on top. However the trick of this position is that the man has to crawl and the woman lifts her pelvis towards the penis to get penetrated. He remains in this position while the woman does all the work.

Chapter 4. Emotional and Physical Intimacy

Intimacy, in a general sense, is defined as mutual openness and vulnerability between two people. There are different ways in which you can give and receive openness and vulnerability in a relationship.

Emotional

Emotional intimacy is the ability to express oneself in a mature and open manner, leading to a deep emotional connection between people. Saying things like "I love you" or "you are very important to me" are examples of this. It is also the ability to respond in a mature and open way when someone expresses themselves to you by saying things like "I'm sorry" or "I love you too." This type of open and vulnerable dialogue leads to an emotional connection. In order for a deep emotional connection to form, there must be a mutual willingness to be vulnerable and open with one's deeper thoughts and feelings. This is where this type of emotional intimacy comes from.

Physical

Physical intimacy is the type that most people think of when they hear the term "intimacy", and it is the kind that we will be most concerned with in this book, as it is the type of intimacy that includes sex and all activities related to sex. It also involves other non-sexual types of physical contact, such as hugging and kissing. Physical intimacy can be found in close friendships or familial relationships where hugging and kisses on the cheek are common, but it is most often found in romantic relationships.

Physical intimacy is the type of intimacy involved when people are trying to make each other orgasm. Physical intimacy is almost always required for orgasm. Physical intimacy doesn't necessarily mean that you are in love with the person you are having sex with; it just means that you are doing something intimate with another person in a physical way.

How to Increase Intimacy

For a romantic relationship to be successful, there must be several forms of intimacy shared between the partners. Without a combination of all of the forms of intimacy, there is nothing that sets a romantic relationship apart from an everyday friendship.

It is important to communicate about your needs for intimacy with your partner so that they know what is important to you and what you need from them for the relationship to be successful. Further, this must be discussed on a recurring basis since people will grow and change over the course of their relationship and both partners must be aware of the changes in the needs of their romantic partner. This is especially important in a long-term relationship, as being aware of when a person's intimacy needs change is important to maintaining a good level of intimacy and a deep connection. This leads us to the next topic related to intimacy, which is communication.

Communication

Communication is the key in a relationship of any sort, but especially in a romantic relationship. Communicating is the only sure way to know where the other person stands in terms of their thoughts, feelings, and needs. Being able to be vulnerable and open with your emotions is a requirement for any type of intimacy, and this involves being vulnerable and open about your needs for intimacy itself. It is necessary to share oneself with the other person in a relationship. This mutual sharing of yourselves is what will lead to intimacy in the first place as well as an increase in your level of intimacy.

Blindfolded Exploration

A great way to rediscover your partner's body, especially if you feel like you already know it so well is to explore it blindfolded. You can make this a sexy exploration with the blindfold being almost BDSM-like or leading up to something bigger, or you can keep it cute and loving, whichever style best suits you both. After setting the mood and taking your partner's clothes off, get them to blindfold you. Have them lie down in a comfortable position and begin gently exploring their bodies with your hands. You can use massage oil if you want but focus on the exploration. Exploring their body without your sight will give you a new perspective of the body you thought you knew so well. You will be able to feel the details you overlooked for all these years, and once you discover them, you will have a new image in front of your eyes every time you look at them afterward. You can take turns doing this, having the partner that is being explored lying down and enjoying the sensations, or you can do it together at the same time if you wish. With both of you naked and blindfolded, get into a comfortable position that allows all of your arms to be free to move and leaves your body open. Lying down on your sides face-to-face is a good position for this, and you can switch sides partway through if you wish. To start out, focus on exploring each other with your hands and avoid focusing too heavily on any one part of their body, we want to discover it all. Take your time though and move gently. Once you have been doing this for a little, you can start to kiss each other, still blindfolded, and progress to wherever you want to go. All of these sensations will prove to be different when blindfolded. You will have a heightened physical sensation because your vision is not there. If you wish to have sex, try it blindfolded as well. Oral sex and penetrative sex with a blindfold will surely help you rediscover their body even further. As the woman, try giving your partner a hand job while blindfolded. You will feel all of the curves and nuances to his penis and see it in a new way perhaps. As the man, give your partner a vulva massage and find her clitoris with your eyes covered. This will help you to find it ever after without even looking. Feel around gently and discover everything between her legs. Eventually, you can slip a finger inside of her and discover her spot and what it feels like. Even though you never actually see it, having a blindfold on will enhance your physical sensations in general, so touching inside of her will feel different than it does when you have your vision.

Best Positions for Intimacy

30. The Mermaid

The male lies on his back, ready to do some lifting with his partner. With his legs bent and spread apart, he acts as a makeshift cradle for his lover. On the other hand, the woman sits atop this cradle with her back facing the man. Her legs are either kept together or spread depending on their difference in size. She keeps her legs raised into the air as she is supported by the man beneath her.

31. The Shuttle

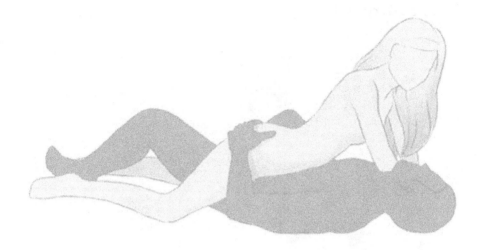

The man lies on his back as he serves as a cushion for the woman who lies above him. Instead of spreading his legs, he keeps his legs slightly apart only to entertain one leg from his partner. The female then faces her partner and cradles her crotch on one of the outstretched legs of her lover.

Benefits: This position allows for eye-to-eye contact and kissing during lovemaking.

32. The Aquarius

The man takes the woman by the waist and claims her as he is standing on his knees. With his legs together, he pleases his lover as he holds her lower half higher than her back. The woman lays on her back, appreciating her lover and his efforts from the surface of the bed.

Tips: She may use her hands to support her back or hold hands with her lover as they engage in congress

33. The Candle

As the name implies, both lovers come into the shape of a candle with the tops aflame with passion for each other. The male stands behind his lover as he claims her from between her buttocks. His hands are free to satisfy her other parts such as her navel or breasts or neck

Tips: He also has the option of kissing the neck or using his hands to guide his lover's face to his for kisses. The female stands in front as she enjoys her man. She may use her hands to caress from the back as well as cling to his sides.

34. The Tulip

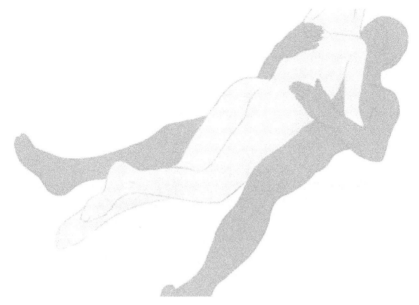

As the lovers face each other, the man lies on his back as he serves as a cradle for his woman. With his legs apart, he welcomes her weight onto him as he pleases her.

On the other hand, the woman lies atop her lover with her legs together, making for a tighter union that brings more pleasure to the male.

Tips: With both sets of hands free, the lovers may choose to caress and rub each other to heighten pleasure.

35. The Swing

The woman sits atop her lover with her back facing him. She sits like a queen on her throne with her legs crossed. Similar to the earlier position, this also makes for a tighter congress and is ideal for unequal levels of lovers. The man makes use of his arms and hands to act as support for the weight of his lover as she sits.

Tips: The woman may choose to press her hands onto her lovers' chest or the bed behind him for support. The male can rock his lover forward to back as if on a wing, changing the dynamics of the lovemaking.

36. The Storm

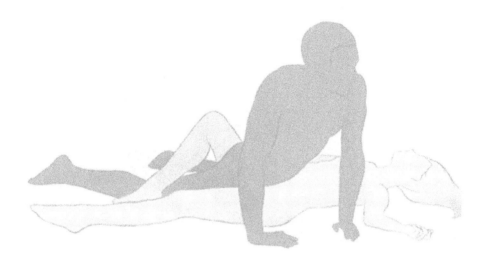

With the woman lying on her back, she raises one knee by bending to create a tunnel through which her lover may squeeze. With the man's torso aligned with his lover's crotch, he may please her while her lifted leg pins him in place.

Tips: the complete upper sections of both parties are free to add more variety to the lovemaking.

37. The Binding

Interestingly, this position has become quite the favorite in pornographic settings due to the amount of exposure this position brings. Here, the couple engages a spooning position wherein both parties lie on the bed while the male claims his lover from behind. In this particular position, the female raises her leg closest to the ceiling to allow for a better congress.

Tips: the man can choose to hold his lover's leg up with his hand or use them to pleasure the other areas of his willing partner.

38. The Riding

With the man lying on the bed, he serves as the ride for his lover. On the other hand, the woman squats atop the man, exposing herself and their union to him.

In this setting, the male has both hands free to support his lover as she is in an unusual position. His goal here is to keep her balanced as she dictates the tempo of the congress. From the same position, the woman uses her legs to either push her up and down or rock her back and forth on top of her lover.

Tips: It is also to be noted that both lovers should be facing each other in this position and should make the most of this exposure through kissing and other forms of flirting.

39. The Fire

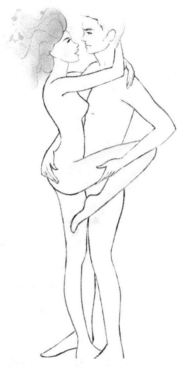

Speaking with a more aggressive tone, the lovers engage in a standing position. This usually takes place at the onset of sexual congress as lovers begin to explore each other's bodies. Here, the woman faces her man as she stands up and lifts her thigh so that it rests on the waist of her lover. In that position, the male takes hold of this thigh and ensures that it is clasped to his side as he pleasures his partner.

Tips: With one hand free, the man may choose to cradle the back of his woman or use it to please her breasts. He may also use his arms to bring the face of his lover closer to him for a kiss.

40. The Casket

With the male kneeling on one knee, he will act as a pillar on which his lover will hang her legs. The woman joins her lover in a unique position; with her ankles upon her lover's shoulders. One ankle each shoulder in that case. She then uses her arms to prop herself up as she is being pleasured by her lover.

41. The Dangling

The female bends over the table with her behind exposed to her lover. In this position, she is pleasured from behind as she lays flat on the table with her legs dangling off the edge.

In this template, the woman is rendered immobile because she has no anchor on which to place her feet as she is pleasured. She becomes a complete receptor of pleasure as her lover does as he pleases.

Tips: Instead of resorting to the bedroom, a couple may choose a higher surface such as a table or a counter top. Be sure to use a blanket or a towel to keep matters clean.

42. The Locked Candle

Also a standing position like the Candle, this variation has the lovers facing each other as they stand. Here, the male must raise his leg on a stool or chair to keep his thigh up for his lover to sit on.

From there, the woman will wrap her legs around her lover and enjoy him as he lifts her up and tends to her needs.

Tips: In some cases, couples may not need to use a stool or chair if the male is strong enough to carry his own lover. This may be the case in higher unions.

43. The Intimate Spoon

This is a permutation of the earlier-mentioned spoon position which allows for more options during coitus. From a spoon position, the male may guide his lover to rotate to a certain angle that will end in his lover lying on her back with their legs alternating each other. This will show as the woman with one leg over the man's thigh while he is still within her.

Tips: With the woman and man perpendicular to each other, they may engage in kissing or fondling or any other of the arts mentioned in this manual as they are no longer in a spoon.

44. The Strong Lotus

With the man standing on his knees on the bed, he bends his legs to act as a cushion for his lover's bottom. Here, the woman places herself on his thighs and for him to tend to her. She keeps her legs outstretched as she sits on his thighs. The thighs will not provide enough support for the woman though, and she should wrap her arms around her lover's neck and the man should support his lover's back with his hands to keep her in place.

Tips: Interestingly, this template can also be done in a standing position should the male be of ample physical aptitude.

45. The Mantis

This is another position meant for the bed. Here, the man lies on his back as he faces his lover who is right on top of him. The woman rests her breasts upon his face as her arms and elbows act as support on the bed next to the man's shoulders. With both legs bent, the man lifts his torso to pleasure his lover who has her legs bent backwards.

Tips: The man may use his arms to hold onto her ankles or feet to keep them bent and he pleasures her. Lovers are in each other's faces and may kiss or the male may nibble on his lover's breasts as he pleasures her. All the woman has to focus on is to keep her elbows anchored to the bed to keep her upright.

46. The Stargazer

The male lies on his back while his lover is on top of him with her back facing him. From this point, the male must guide his lover's back as she leans backwards so that her back touches his chest. This must not be done abruptly, especially if the lovers are already joined. Once the back of the woman meets the chest of the male, both lovers now face the sky that brings the name of the template.

Tips: The additional skin contact will prove to be pleasurable for both lovers as they enjoy coital congress.

Benefits: Given this position, both pairs of arms are free to explore each other.

47. The Lazy 2

The man kneels with his buttocks resting on his heels and supports himself with his arms. The woman is lying on the bed with her head on the pillow and her back well stretched out. To allow optimal penetration, raise your partner's tight thighs. It can stimulate other areas by dispensing stroking the breasts and the mount of Venus.

Benefits: Particularly sexy and exciting, this position offers deep penetration and offers partners the opportunity to observe each other.

48. The Vertical Hug

The man lies on his stomach, keeping his legs slightly apart. The woman lies on him on his stomach, letting herself be penetrated and stretching her legs until they are completely extended in the middle of his legs.

Benefits: It is an excellent position for constant contact between partners and for shallow penetration.

49. Passionate Proposal

The position of the passionate proposal requires a little practice and a lot of will. Kneeling face to face, the man puts his foot firmly planted on the ground in front of him (as if he were making a marriage proposal) and the woman puts her right foot on the ground, climbing over his kneeling leg.

Tips: The penetration can be done by leaning forward towards the planted feet, making lunges, as if you were dancing slowly.

Chapter 5. The Orgasm

Super orgasm

For many people, when it comes to lovemaking, the orgasm isn't the cherry on top. It's the entire sundae. They treat foreplay and intercourse as if there were playing poker, and if they play their cards right, they win the pot and cash those chips in for a mind-blowing, body quivering orgasm.

What if they don't climax? Well, then they treat the whole experience as though they won the pot only to discover the chips can't be cashed in. They're stuck with two handfuls of cheap plastic. Everyone can agree that orgasms feel amazing. It's a sure sign that all the elements in lovemaking came together correctly to give that partner a moment of ecstasy.

As great as they are, it's a huge mistake to make that the goal of lovemaking, especially when practicing the Kama Sutra. When practicing the techniques, the experience shouldn't be a judge on whether or not one or both partners experienced orgasms. In fact, they shouldn't even be basing it on how close they came to climaxing. Orgasms can be very elusive, especially for women. Sometimes it might take more time than they have. Sometimes thinking about it makes it difficult actually to have it. Sometimes, it doesn't happen because it just didn't happen.

Male Orgasm Basics

The male orgasm is something that most people have witnessed or seen if they have ever watched any sort of porn or heard about it in the media. The male orgasm is made out to be extremely simple and easy to achieve, but in this section, we are going to examine it in more detail and break it down into more specific parts.

To start, are you aware that there are different types of male orgasms? If you are a male, you are likely aware of this, but if you are a female, you may not be. The term male orgasm includes any and every type of orgasm that involves the male's genitals.

Orgasm and Ejaculation

Ejaculation and orgasm for males are two distinct events, even though they most often happen at the same time. This fact makes them often misunderstood, as many think that ejaculation is a sign of orgasm. If orgasm occurs and ejaculation occurs at the same time, this is called an ejaculatory orgasm.

There is another type of orgasm, one that happens when ejaculation does not. As you likely guessed, this type is called a non-ejaculatory orgasm. This is sometimes called a dry orgasm as well, and this type is also very normal. A man can achieve orgasm without ejaculation, and this still counts as an orgasm.

How to Stimulate the Prostate to Achieve Orgasm

Once you have found the prostate, you can begin to massage this area and let the sensations build gently. Keep going like this and find out what type of movements or pressure feels best. As you continue to stimulate it, let the pleasure make until the point of orgasm. When you are comfortable with this spot, try having your partner encourage it for you. Having someone else's hands touch it for you will feel different than your own, and with your free hand, you can turn yourself and your partner on in other ways.

The prostate is sometimes referred to as the male G-Spot. It has many similar properties to the female G-Spot, such as the way that you can find it and how it needs t to be stimulated to reach orgasm. We will learn about the female orgasm in the following section.

Female Orgasm Basics

To make a woman orgasm, you will need to know and understand the female body, including all of the places where, when stimulated, a woman will feel pleasure and maybe even orgasm. Whether you are a female yourself or you are a male with a female partner, both sexes can benefit from learning more about the female body.

How to Stimulate the Clitoris to Achieve Orgasm

Once you have found the clitoris, you will then be able to stimulate it to achieve orgasm. Begin by gently placing two fingers on it and putting a bit of pressure. Rub it by moving your fingers in small circles-making sure to be gentle. Continue to do this, and she should begin to get more aroused the more you do this. By rubbing the clitoris, you will be able to stimulate the entire clitoris, even the part of it that you cannot see, and this will cause the woman to start to become wet in her vaginal area for her body to prepare for sex.

How to Stimulate the G-Spot to Achieve Orgasm

To give a woman pleasure by stimulating her G-Spot, you will need to press on it over and over again until she reaches orgasm. The G-Spot needs to receive continued and consistent stimulation for the pleasure to build enough for her to reach orgasm. This can be done using your fingers, a penis, or sex toys of a variety of sorts.

Since a woman can have two different types of orgasms, one from stimulating the clitoris and a different one from penetration or hitting the G-spot, this could be why a woman can reach orgasm during oral sex, or by having her clitoris stimulated, but has trouble reaching the same level of pleasure during penetrative sex. In many positions, the G-spot is not stimulated by the man's penis, and this can result in the woman having some amount of pleasure, but not enough to reach orgasm. For a great experience as a couple, knowing what makes the woman feel great is paramount.

Chapter 6. Kama Sutra Positions for Male Orgasms

50. "The Blow of the Bull" Role

The man's penis actually covers the woman's obvious vulva. Her thighs are up to the degree of the man's shoulders, whose plunges deeply and forcefully into her so she can experience his member's dimension and length all the better. The lady can stroke the man's buttocks with her fingers all through "The Bull's Blast" phase. The strong thrusts of the man determine the growing sexual strength of the lady alongside the spine.

51. "The Concealed Door" Role

The man lies to his wife. She holds his legs, equipped to take him up to the hilt. He insinuates himself softly and profoundly rooted internal of her, cuddling her there, stroking her back, thighs, breasts. She stretches her legs and opens them barely to yield herself to the wants of her lover even in addition so that she can give her vulva to the glans and penis shaft fully.

Even in the same role, the male lover can also have enjoyable with his lover's anal opening, if he knows she loves anal penetrations. In this way, the woman can loosen up in the first-rate possible way, and the man has complete manipulate over his penis' penetration into the moist and confined opening that she gives him with love and trust. He holds her by her thighs, can bite her throat, and brush over her breasts with his hands, whilst thrusting ever deeper. The man's urge is entire in both cases and of a lengthy length.

Benefits: This position is sufficient to bring up the sexual strength and sublimate it in pure love. To acquire this extended emotion-pure love, the enthusiasts do not have to focal point on the genital gratification throughout this phase. Still, they have to center of attention their attention on the region of the coronary heart and turn out to be aware of the flying feeling this segment creates.

52. "The Cares of the BUD" Function

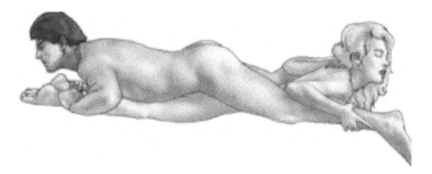

Lying on the floor, legs interlacing, the man and woman flip to every other with their backs. However, for certain men, whose brief and thick penis can solely be flexed with difficulty, the specific effect of this role can be incredibly painful. In the continuation of this role, the woman, who now retains her balance with one arm going through her lover and who is supported on the physique of the man, is solely titillated by means of the glans at the entrance of her vagina. It is, of course, simply foreplay to deeper coitus. The guy inserts his erect penis into the vagina by using softly shifting to one side. Now the vagina is geared up to acquire it in full.

Benefits: The function is suitable for these fanatics who are beginners in the art of regulating sexual energy. "The caress of the bud" position provides lovers with the opportunity of becoming more aware of the

79

degree of gratification and, as a consequence, it through stopping the movement when they experience that they are shut to the climax.

53. Face to Face

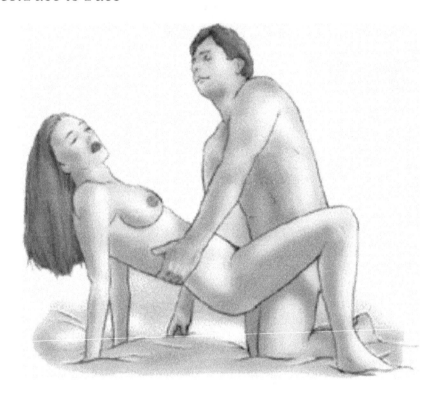

Holding on her arms and soles, the female raises her pelvis to allow the man to insert his penis into her vagina. Being kneeled, he may seize his lover's waist with one or both hands. The female should shift her pelvis softly, matching her step with the coming and going of the man's movements. To take up the full erectile length of her lover's cock, she has to unfold more often than not her legs.

Tips: If the man feels close to the ejaculatory orgasm, he has to end shifting and center of attention his interest in the location of the heart to sublimate the sexual energy. This can be achieved for the girl too.

Benefits: This position helps lovers to seem at one another-seeing how their appeal rises and sharing their love.

54. "Driving the Nail Home" Position

Facing her, with his chest pushing on her breasts, the man plunges into the vagina of the girl with full loins thrusts

The female receives him with broadly unfold thighs right up to the hilt. Even if there is consistency between the dimension of the woman's vagina and the dimension of the man's penis, then the woman will attain the cervical-uterine orgasm that is usually for the tantric orgasm. Contrary to all assumptions, the female in this function needs to no longer be passive. She has to hold close the man's buttocks and press his pelvis on hers to assist him in reaching deep into her.

Tips: This position in the art of sexual continence is now not recommended for beginners in view that it encourages the awareness of sexual energy in the genital region.

Benefits: This role favours the entire intimacy of the lovers' genital zones.

55. "The Open Pincer" Role

On her back, the female spreads her legs. Her husband grips her knees, and she's pressured to unfold her legs even further. Having her legs spread like this, she can in no way fight against his invasion. He can explore her to the content of his core-gently with the complete length of his penis or-which will stimulate her urge for food for more-he can aggressively insert and withdraw his member.

Tips: Both lovers ought to pay attention to their attention all through the "Open Pincer" position to direct the fundamental and sexual strength alongside the spine till the crown.

56. "The TOP" Position

"The location of the TOP" is very similar to the missionary position. It makes it handy for the man to enter it without having to withdraw his penis from the vagina of his lover. That is why the fanatics would take the "top" role after the classical one to remain in contact with their genitals. Fans keep in touch with their sexual organs at some point in intercourse, seeing that the intense interplay between fanatics that is initiated throughout the erotic act is no longer disrupted this way.

Within that role, the lady should now not be passive. Through preserving the thighs of the man, she will press his pelvis on hers, supporting him to penetrate deeply into her.

Similar to the position of "Moving the nail home," "The peak" role in the art of sexual continence is not endorsed for beginners as it encourages the concentration of sexual power in the genital region. This is why the man must make gradual movements and middle his attention in the cardiac plexus to regulate the sexual electricity and end the ejaculation.

57. "The TOP" Function - Variant 1

Lying on her back, supported and blanketed via the thighs of the man who penetrates her in a guided press-up, the woman is massaged tightly on the hands, taking up the penis' entire length. This challenge needs to be carried out after the "Head" role to preserve the lovers' sexual organs in touch. At the second, when the man feels close to the ejaculatory climax, he has to pause his moves and sit there for at least 30 seconds to stop ejaculation.

Similar to "the top" position, this position gives each fan intense pleasure, and it favours the accumulation of sexual strength in the genital region.

The fans want to focal point their interest in the center of the forehead to sublimate the sexual electricity. It extends their control energy over the sexual energy.

58. "Driving the Nail Home" Role - Variant 1

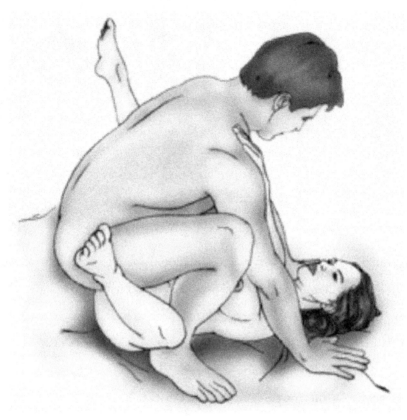

The man plunges into her with deep thrusts, going through her, lying on top of her, aiding himself on his soles. She receives him with tightly spread thighs proper up to the hilt. The man may additionally both cross his pelvis lower back and forth or up and down. Contrary to all assumptions in this function, the female does not have to be passive. She's bought to grasp the man's thighs with her fingers and pull him in opposition to her to attain deeper into her vagina.

When the man feels shut to the ejaculatory orgasm, he ought to pause his movements for a few seconds and focus his interest on the crown to direct the sexual energy through the spine to the crown.

59. "Driving the Nail Home" Role - Variant 2

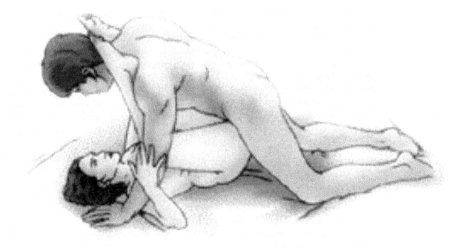

To both lovers, face-to-face roles are enjoyable. They motivate them to seem at every other, to see how their desire mounts and, above all, to share caresses among themselves. The female lies behind her. Facing her, leaning on top of her, the guy plunges with full thrusts of his loins into the woman's vagina. He then places her fingers on his back. The man's erected penis fills up the woman's vagina. The man plunges into her profoundly and firmly with his pelvis, touching her pelvic intimately so that she can sense his member's presence all the better.

In this place, the female is not passive. Holding the man's thighs, she pulls the man's pelvis toward her to reach deeper in his thrusts. The robust thrusts of the man in this position might also provoke the awakening of the Kundalini of the woman. Lovers must discover their effective rhythm, which generates their Kundalini power's awakening.

60. "The TOP" Role - Variant 2

Lying on her back, supported and protected via the thighs of the man who penetrates her in a guided press-up, the woman is firmly massaged on the hands, taking up the whole length of the penis. He reasons his weight to fall on her even further, at the second, when he needs to feel further pleasure. The lady can experience him even more strongly at the equal time.

Tips: Both lovers have to middle their energies in the discipline of the heart to sublimate the sexual electricity into greater refined sorts of energy. When the girl senses that her lover is getting close to the climax, she has to cease the man's actions and press firmly in the center of the brow with her thumb.

Benefits: The "row" role offers both lovers huge pleasure and amplifies the sexual energy. This is why newbie in the art of sexual continence lovemaking need to not to proceed the intercourse with it.

61. "Face to Face" Function - Variant 1

The girl lies on the back, shut to the aspect of the bed. She stretches her legs and puts one on the board. The guy is facing her, mendacity on top of her, and plunges with strong thrusts into the woman's vagina. Two of his legs unfold on the concrete, and the different one is folded.

The girl experiences his lover proper up to the hilt with thighs broadly spread. The man can explore her to the core of his heart-gently with the complete size of his penis, or-which will expand his appetite for more-he can violently insert and withdraw his penis.

Benefits: This role favours the whole intimacy of the lovers' genital zones. That is why the man should quit his motions when he reaches the pre-orgasmic stage and listen to his interest in the cardiac plexus to direct the sexual energy.

Chapter 7. Kama Sutra Positions for Female Orgasms

62. Praying Mantis

The woman will lie down on her back with her legs open. The man will kneel in front of her pelvis and penetrate her. He will take one leg and bring it up slowly to that it points the ceiling. He can then place it on his shoulder or wrap his arm around it.

63. Jugghead

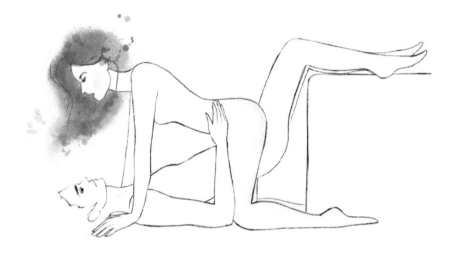

The man is going to lie down either beside a couch or bed while keeping his back on the floor. The man will put his legs up on the bed or sofa. The woman will position herself above the man while being on all fours with an arm and a leg on each side of him. The man is going to lift his lower back and crotch off the floor so he can penetrate you. The woman will sit on his penis and thrust herself back into him.

Tips: The woman can thrust as hard as you want or just let him push into you while you take it easy.

64. Thigh Tide

The man is going to lie down on his back with his legs straight in front of him. He will raise one knee just a bit and put his foot on the bed. The woman is going to face away from the man. She is going to place one knee on either side of the man's bent leg while sitting on his penis. She will raise herself up and down on him.

Tips: She can hold on to the man's leg to help keep her balance.

65. Washing Machine

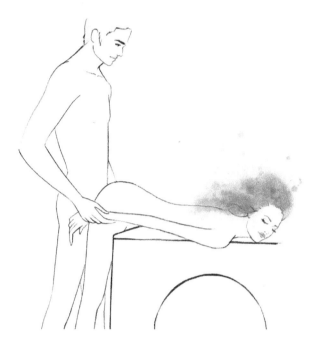

Find a load of dirty clothes and wash them. When the washing machine gets to the spin cycle, the woman will lean over it while keeping her feet on the floor. This puts her pubic region against the vibrating washing machine. The man will penetrate the woman from behind and begin thrusting.

Tips: The only thing the woman needs to do is to lie against the machine and let it and her man do the work.

66. Drill Position

The woman is going to lie down on her back like she is getting ready for the missionary position. The man will be on top of you. The woman will raise her legs and wrap them around his waist.

Tips: To help you keep them around him, cross your ankles. This helps you grip him tighter and pull him to you.

67. Poles Apart

Both the man and woman are going to lie down on their sides. You both will be facing the same way. You aren't going to be lying with your head at his head; you are going to turn around, so your head is at his feet. Basically, you are going to be lying head to feet with your man going the opposite direction. The man will then penetrate you from behind.

68. Side Saddle

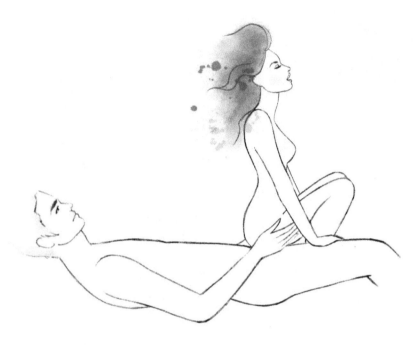

The man is going to lie down, facing up on a bed. He needs to have his rear end on the edge of the bed and his feet are going to be hanging over the edge. His feet should be flat on the floor. He can either spread his legs out or leave them together. The woman will stand over the man keeping her back to him. She can now sit down on his penis. If his legs are closed, she will need to spread her legs. If his legs are open, she will sit on him with her legs together and closed.

69. Pile Driver

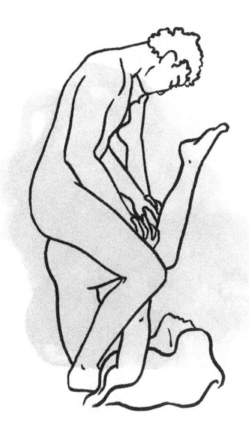

The woman is going to lie on her back and lift her legs in the air. The man is going to grab her ankles and push them slowly up over your head. The woman's lower back is going to come off the bed. If it is comfortable for the man, he will continue pushing your ankles until the only thing still on the bed is just your shoulders. The man will keep one hand on her ankles, so she stays in place. In order to penetrate her, he will have to point his penis down.

Tips: He has to be careful not to hurt himself in this position.

70. Scissors

The woman will lie down on her side with her legs on top of each other. Now she will raise one leg and bend it slightly so the man can get to her vagina easily. The man is going to be lying on his side, too. He will be positioned so that his head is near your feet. He will slide his lower leg under her lower leg near her crotch. Now, he will place his top leg over her lower leg and move closer until he is able to penetrate her.

This places her lower leg in between his legs. The woman will be facing away from the man while he is facing her back. Once he is comfortable, and inside the woman, he will begin thrusting.

71. Speed Bump

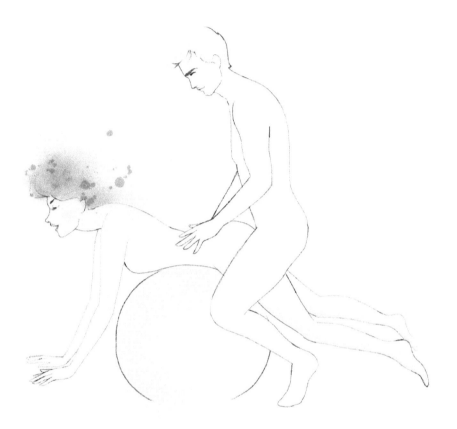

The woman is going to lie on top of the ball on her stomach. She will balance herself by placing her hands in front of her. If it is small, she could place her feet on the ground, too. The man is going to penetrate her from behind. He can control her movement by holding onto her legs or waist.

72. Leg Glider

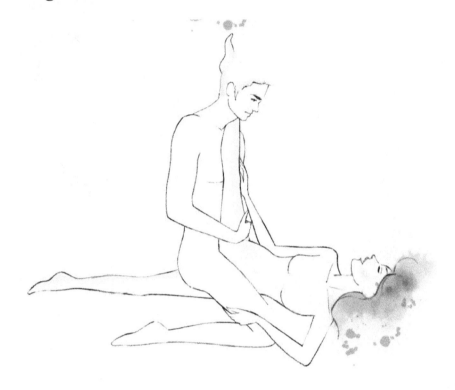

The woman needs to lie on one side. For this example, we are saying your left side. The woman's left leg, arm, and side are going to be on the bed. The woman's right leg will be resting on her left leg, and her right arm will rest on her body. You could also place your hand on the bed to keep yourself steady if you want to. The woman will raise her right leg toward the ceiling while she keeps her left leg on the bed. If she is very flexible, her leg should be pointing at the ceiling. The woman's legs should make a 90-degree angle.

The man will be on his knees, keeping his back straight. He is going to straddle her left leg while supporting her right leg of his chest and shoulder. The man will then penetrate the woman and use her leg to help pull himself forward and back.

73. Flatiron

The woman is going to lie down on her side with her legs together and slightly bent. If she is flexible enough, she can rotate her upper body to slightly face the man. It makes intimacy better. The man will be on his knees and will penetrate from behind.

74. Anvil

The woman should lie down on her back. Don't leave the legs on the bed, but pull them as close as you can to your legs. The man will position himself over her. He isn't going to rest on the elbows but rest on his hands. Your man can help you position your legs so your ankles are resting on his shoulders. The man will then begin thrusting in and out as fast or slow as he wants.

75. Butterfly

The woman is going to lie down on the bed or table on her back and lift her hips. The man will come up and penetrate the woman. The woman can then place her ankles over the man's shoulder or just place then against his chest or at his waist. Just find a position that works best for you.

Benefits: In this position, the penetration will be extremely deep for her.

76. Crisscross

The woman is going to lie down on her back on a table or bed. She is going to raise her legs and point them toward the ceiling. The man is going to come up to her and enter her. After he has penetrated her, she will keep her legs straight and then cross them slowly.

Tips: It might be easiest to just cross her legs at the ankle. If this is too hard, you could just place them on his chest.

77. Sandwich

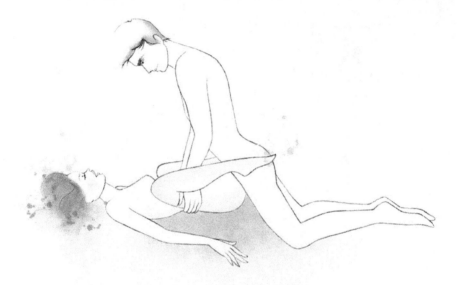

The woman will lie down on her back, and the man will penetrate her, just like in the missionary position. Instead of putting her legs on the bed, she will bring them up toward her chest while leaving them open. The man's arms are going to be around her shoulders. He will now bring them down and place them under her knees and lift them to change up the angle of penetration.

78. Frog Leap

The woman will get into position by squatting and bending at the knees while leaning forward, so her hands are on the floor to keep her balanced. You are literally going to look like a frog getting ready to jump. The man will get behind the woman on his knees and penetrates her just like regular doggy style sex.

The woman might have to adjust how wide she spreads her legs until she finds a position that feels best for her. From that point, she will just lean back into the man and thrust into him. Until you get used to this position, you can do this in front of the bed so you can rest your weight on the bed rather than her hands.

Benefits: This position gives much deeper penetration just by changing the angle of your back slightly. Your hands are also free to stimulate your clitoris.

79. Bassett Hound

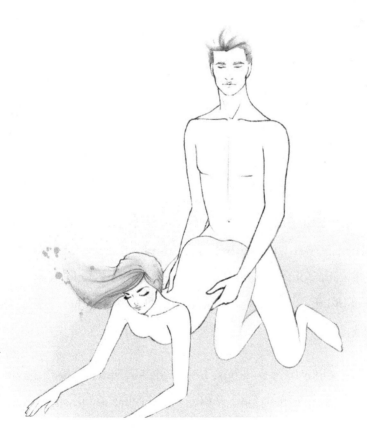

The woman is going to get on all fours (hands and knees). Then lower herself by spreading her knees out more and pushing her butt back. This lowers the waist. Come down off your hands and rest on your forearms, and spread them out some to bring your chest lower. The man will penetrate her from behind while on his knees. He might have to spread his legs to get as low as the woman.

80. Stairway to Heaven

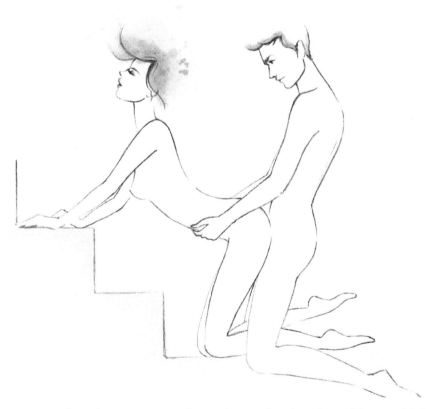

The woman is going to get on the stairs on her hands and knees. Make sure her knees are on a lower step than her hands. It will be up to her as to how far she wants to stretch. Since the man is going to penetrate from behind, he might find it hard to get his position right. It is going to take some experimenting to get your positions just right.

Tips: Since this position is done on a staircase, you might want to make sure you do it on the carpet or put some pillows down.

81. Final Furlong

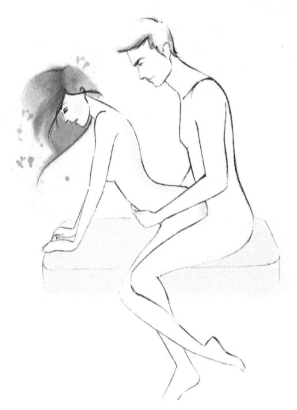

The man and woman are going to straddle the piece of furniture while facing in the same direction. The man will sit behind you. The woman will lean slightly so he will be able to penetrate her easily. When he is inside of her, he will be able to hold you close and begin thrusting in and out.

Tips: The hardest part of this position is finding the right piece of furniture. You are both going to be sitting in the exact same position. The best things would be a footrest or wide stool that will hold both of you.

Chapter 8. Sex Toys

Sex Toys for Him

Cock Ring

A cock ring was originally designed to keep a man's penis harder for a longer period of time. It does this because it is a ring made of metal that sits at the base of a man's penis, which helps to keep the blood flow inside of the penis for longer, which maintains an erection. These cock rings can be as tight or as loose as the man is comfortable with, as they come in a variety of sizes. This will also increase the man's pleasure as he will last longer.

Flashlight

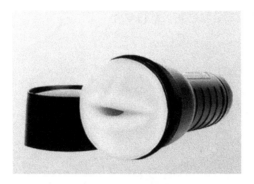

This toy works by simulating a vagina or a mouth because of the way it looks and feels. Essentially it is a toy that can be disguised as a flashlight because when it has the lid on, it looks very much like a flashlight. When you take off the lid, however, it looks like the opening of a vagina or mouth made of silicone. The man will insert his penis into the flashlight and have penetrative sex with it as if it were a vagina or a mouth. The inside of the tube is texturized for added sensation. The soft silicone will feel similar to the skin of a woman, and this is why men find it a turn on to use this for masturbation rather than just their hand.

Sex Toys for Her

Clitoral Vibrator

Clitoral vibrators are small and compact, portable, and easy to use. This type of vibrator is turned on with the push of a button, and then you can hold it to your clitoris for quick and intense clitoral pleasure in a way like nothing else. Having something that is designed to be used on your clitoris that is also vibrating at speeds much higher than your hands could ever reach will be quite a new sensation, but one that you won't soon forget and will be quite eager to have again.

Bunny Ears Vibrator

There is another type of vibrator that is a little larger than a clitoral vibrator, and that also has an extra protruding piece on the side of it which can be inserted into the vagina so that you can have both vaginal penetration (so that you can stimulate your G-Spot) as well as vibrating, clitoral stimulation. This type is called a bunny ears vibrator since the portion that you insert into your vagina looks a little bit like bunny ears. With this shape, you can feel both of these types of pleasure at the same time! This will be a new world of pleasure for you as you may never have had both your clitoris and your G-Spot stimulated at the same time.

Vibrating Dildo

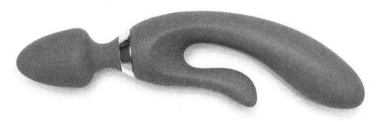

This specific type of dildo is a sort of hybrid, as it can act as a vibrator as well. This is usually done by way of a small bullet-shaped vibrator that is inserted into it. This type of vibrator allows you to have penetration with vibration. Because of this, the G-Spot can be stimulated and vibrated on at the same time, which will lead to intense pleasure.

Dildo

Dildos can be used by a woman alone while masturbating by being inserted into the vagina to stimulate her G-Spot. While doing this, you can also massage your clitoris with your other hand, or you can stick with the vaginal stimulation on its own.

A dildo can be used in the vagina or the anus, whichever you prefer, and you can use the same dildo for both of these places, so you don't need to buy two. If you want to use your dildo during a solo session, you can insert it into your anus in a similar way as you would insert it into your vagina. Just be sure that when switching between the anus and the vagina, you thoroughly clean the dildo and/or your hands to prevent the chance of an infection.

Sex Positions and Sex Toys: How to Correctly Combine Them

Sex toys can make familiar postures vivid and memorable. But what intimate things to apply in certain positions? How to use them so that they help, rather than interfere with the process? You can use sex toys in any position, in different circumstances. But somewhere, a mini-vibrator that works silently and does not attract attention will be more appropriate, but somewhere a massager that connects to the network would be more useful. When used, the sensations will be different, and it's interesting! With intimate little things you will never get bored in bed, even after 10 years of living together.

82. Missionary Position with Sex Toys

The classic position for sex can be varied. A girl can widely spread her legs, hug them around the partner or even throw them on his shoulders. At the same time, a sex toy is able to additionally massage the erogenous zones of the partners. Choose a model to stimulate the clitoris, massage the genitals of both partners, or use butt plugs for pleasant sensations in very tender places.

What sex toys to use in a missionary position?

- Vibrator for the clitoris.

It is used to increase her arousal, to bring closer the onset of orgasm or to help her experience several peaks of pleasure at once. The clitoral stimulator is set to the desired point, it can be hold it with your hands, and with your fingers to regulate the impact. With a vibrating little thing, you can draw some kind of drawing on the clitoris, but the vacuum model does not move. It is the wave or vacuum stimulation that guarantees the orgasm.

- Vibrator for a couple.

Used directly during sex. One part of the toy is placed in the woman's vagina, the second touch her clitoris. In this case, the toy does not interfere with the penetration of the man. And wavering is felt by both partners. For her, there is stimulation of the clitoris, entrance to the vagina and the G-spot; for him there is a massage of the glans of the penis. The more modes the toy has, the more sensations partners can experience. And ideally, if the device is controlled from a remote control or from a smart phone, then you do not need to reach for it.

- An erection ring with vibration.

An erection ring with vibration is put on the penis in an excited state and prevents the outflow of sperm, as a result, a man cannot quickly finish. It does not cause discomfort, but it lengthens the intercourse by 20-30%. Typically, this device has also a motor built into it, which, in a missionary position, touches the woman's clitoris. Sensations of vibration enhance her experiences, increase excitement and bring orgasm closer. This sex toy can help a couple experience a simultaneous orgasm.

83. Doggy Style with Sex Toys

Position "on your knees" is very convenient for using sex toys. A girl can lean on one palm or elbow, while the second hand is free to keep an intimate thing. And you can try the vibrators that are mounted on the body, they are used without hands. Additional stimulation of the clitoris in this position is recommended, it is she who will increase the number of her orgasms several times. And a sex toy will be appropriate if you practice both vaginal and anal sex.

119

What sex toys to use in a doggy style pose?

- Vibrator for couples.

The universal thing for any poses. Vibrates and massages point G and the clitoris of the girl. And there are models that also rotate. There is the submersible piece that moves in a circle, massaging both partners. A unique thing is a vibrator, which acts on the clitoris not with vibration, but with airwaves. With such an object, her first orgasm will happen in 1-2 minutes. You don't have to hold vibrators for couples with your hands, they do not fall out during the process.

- Double penetration nozzle.

In doggy style, it is worthwhile to realize the dream of many - to plunge into both of its holes at the same time. And for this, you do not need a third partner, just buy a special nozzle. The removable phallus is fixed to the penis and scrotum of the man, and it seems that he has two penises at once. The movements in both holes are synchronized, which causes a very pleasant experience. The nozzles are always small in diameter so that the girl does not experience pain or discomfort.

- Mini vibrator.

The small vibrator can simply be driven through the body. Additional breast caresses will please her, but it will be most interesting when the toy touches the clitoris. Of course, the lady will have to keep such a thing in her hands, but then she can easily regulate the force, vibration intensity and range of motion. The ideal solution is a vibrator with three shaking legs that can "hug" her nipples, clitoris or even ears.

84. "Spoons" Or Side Positions with Sex Toys

The laziest pose is lying on the side. It is convenient to have sex when both partners are tired. Sometimes it's nice to start the morning with her. But even in this position, sex toys will be appropriate. As always, a vibrator is suitable for couples, it is universal. But you can also try a massager, it can caress different parts of the body. An anal vibrator or even strapon will help to get aroused.

What sex toys to use in a pose "on the side"?

- Vacuum or wave stimulator.

Vacuum or wave stimulator is a clitoral sex toy guaranteeing her pleasure. The first orgasm occurs within 1-2 minutes. The whole secret is in the special vibrations of the air, which involve even the deepest nerve endings. A sex toy just leans against her body, you do not need to make any movements with it. And she is immediately feeling pleased. And you can combine the effect with penetration, but then she keeps the stimulator herself, it will be more convenient.

- Intimate massager

This is a sex toy for caressing any external erogenous zones. They can touch the back, chest, perineum and genitals. It's worth starting with the gentle point touches of the nipples, then the inner side of the hips. If you need to increase her sensations, then stimulate the clitoris, if his, then apply a massager to the scrotum. The thing is very practical, it will help not only in sex, but also support after a hard day or serious physical exertion. You can massage your back, neck, legs and other parts of the body.

- Anal vibrator

Additional anal stimulation is very exciting. Once you put the plug, turn on its movement, and everything seems completely new. And even the pose of "Spoon" will suddenly sparkle with new colors. At the same time, she can use an anal sex toy, then the sensations will be greater for both: the vagina is smaller in size, and the vibrations are felt by both partners. Or he can insert a cork, but for a lady it will not bring additional pleasure.

85. Sitting Sex with Sex Toys

Sitting sex is practiced by many couples because you can implement it on different surfaces. It is convenient to sit on a bed or on a sofa, you can even seat on a table or window sill. And with all options, sex toys will be great helpers. A clitoral stimulator, a massager or even an electric stimulator is worth a try. The possibility to look into each other's eyes will allow you to choose the right rhythm.

What sex toys to use in a sitting position?

- Anatomical massager

A convenient thing that can be located between the bodies. The main impact is on the clitoris of the girl, but you can also pick up the massager and start driving along the neck, back, or other parts of the body. An ideal model that repeats the bends of the body without obstructing the usual movements. A lot of modes, a waterproof case and a quiet motor will not let you get bored.

- Clitoral vibrator

Pleasant stimulation of the most tender point of the body, she will like it. So that the bodies do not move away from each other, we recommend taking a mini vibrator for the clitoris. Gradually, you can increase the speed of frictions and the vibration power of a sex toy, so that the finale is simply enchanting. Of course, this thing will help exactly the girl to have fun, but sometimes this is what is required in the couple.

- Vibrator for couples

Modern models do not just massage the genitals, they can become a source of unprecedented emotions. After all, vibrators are now synchronized with smartphones. Using the application, you can make a sex toy move to the beat of your favorite melody, and you can feel the music inside! Also, inventing your own vibration modes is available, and there can be infinitely many of them.

- Electrical stimulator.

The form of an electric stimulator can be any: from phallic to unusual. There are even gloves with electrical stimulation. The impact occurs in

123

small discharges of current. It is easy to adjust the impact force, wavelength and repetition rate. Light impacts are like tickling, strong ones resemble pulsation. The application is safe, but it is important to monitor the feelings of the partner. If you want to play on the verge of pleasure and pain, electrical stimulators will help!

86. Sex with Sex Toys in a Cowgirl Position

When a woman is on top, she can help herself cum with her fingers, stimulating the clitoris. But you can do this with a vibrator. Again, you can use a vibrator that is suitable for couples, and also vibro-bullets, massagers and clitoral stimulants. And so that he does not finish quickly, you should buy an erection ring with vibration. For the use of sex toys, this is the most convenient position, and any of the partners can switch speeds.

What sex toys to use in the pose "cowgirl"?

- Vibro-bullet

A vibrating bullet is a vibrator no larger than a finger. In length, it rarely reaches more than 8 cm, the diameter is also insignificant. Most often used to caress the outer zones, rarely immersed in the body. It fits easily between bodies, does not interfere with movement. At the same time, it does not cause jealousy in the partner, because it visually looks harmless, does not resemble the phallus. But at the same time, it can work at different speeds, have a very strong motor. The control can be buttons, from a control panel with a cord or with a remote control.

- Massager for intimate caresses

It is very convenient to use a massager in the position of a cowgirl. It can even be put between bodies and left, it is not always required to fixate it. Both a man or woman can hold it, both options are comfortable. Which massager is right for you? Any! Even the largest will caress the clitoris perfectly. But if it is very large, tilting for a kiss will be uncomfortable for her, but these are trifles.

- Vibrating erection ring.

In this position, the ring can be used not only in the classic version, when the vibrating element is in front, but also when it is located near the scrotum. Of course, the lady will feel it only with deep penetration of the penis in the vagina, and in the area of the perineum, but not on the clitoris. But it's worth a try, most likely that you will get pleasure out of it.

- Butt plug

Anal toys complement intimacy in a pose when the woman is on top. But you can choose not just a cork, but anal rhinestones. This is a bung with a beautiful crystal at the base. If a girl sits with her back to her partner, then he will see not only her body, but also a charming stone in her anus. By the way, with the help of such a cork it is easy to prepare for anal sex.

87. Sex in the 69 Position with Sex Toys

It is also worth using sex toys for oral sex. They help take a break if your neck, lips or tongue are tired. And they help in reaching the finish line quicker, which is very helpful. You can use intimate things with alternating caresses or in the 69 pose. What is suitable for such an experiment? Any vibrators and massagers, and if desired, an artificial penis can be inserted into it.

What sex toys to choose for oral sex?

- Classical shape vibrator.

They can touch any zone, intimate too. It will replace hands and lips to give time to rest. But if you continue oral caresses, and the vibrator touches other parts of the body, the sensations will be three-dimensional, more voluminous. They can be used by both man and woman. And you can even take two vibrators to make it more interesting.

- Massager for tender places.

Any massager will also be appropriate. As soon as they touch his scrotum, the emotions will be completely new. You can also caress the anus with a massager, but it is important not to immerse the device inside, but to move it from the outside, where the maximum number of nerve endings is. You even can find such massager, which also heats besides vibration! A heated vibrator will make every touch very enjoyable. But do not be afraid, it will not burn, its maximum temperature is 48 degrees.

- Ben Wa balls for her.

If you want to give her more sensations during oral caresses, we recommend immersing something in her vagina. The inside presence of the item will increase arousal. Use sterilized and certified proper vaginal balls. This is not just a useful exercise machine for strengthening muscles and preventing dozens of diseases, it is also a thing for pleasure. Balls can be with and without vibration, with a displaced center of gravity, of different diameters and weights.

Chapter 9. Oral Sex Techniques

Best Kama Sutra Oral Sex Positions for Him (Emily Sorensen)

88. Man Standing, Woman Kneeling

This is one of the most popular and classic oral sex positions for men because it lets them watch their partner perform blowjob while she is on her knees in front of him. It gives the man a good view, and he can even use his hand to guide the back of her head and thrust his penis into her mouth. This is a good position for the lady because it makes her neck long and nice, which is good for deep-throating, not choking

89. The Face-off

The woman lies on her back with her head comfortably resting on a pillow. The man then goes up to her face and rest his knees and then bring his genitals towards her face and mouth. The woman can then suck and lick his genitals.

90. Sideways 69

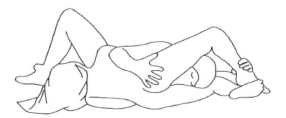

Sideways 69 is another variety of 69 where the couple is lying on their sides rather than one on top and one on base. This position can ease worry from supporting body weight, particularly if both have current ailments around knee or back issues. Simply be cautious with your legs! You may need to make sense of an agreeable leg position before getting into the action. It's just similar to the normal 69; then again, you both lay on your side. Consider making a yin and yang.

91. Corkscrew

The man is going to stand while you kneel in front of him. Hold the base of the penis in both hands. Place his penis in your mouth and tilt your head from side to side as you work up and down their penis.

Best Kama Sutra Oral Sex Positions for Her

92. The 69 Position – A Classic with a Twist

The 69 is a classic sex position most couples would have either heard about, or no doubt tried themselves several times. Traditionally, the 69 got its name because of the way our bodies are positioned when we perform this move. Couples look exactly like the number 69, with partners facing each other in an inverted fashion. In this move, both partners will start by lying on their sides, facing each other but not directly. One partner's head will be towards the top of the bed, the other at the bottom. As you bring your bodies together, your face gets closer to your partner's genitals.

The 69 is one of the best equal side-by-side sex positions you can perform. It gives you a good view of your partner's genitals (which turn you on), and you're both in control of pleasuring the other. Mutually giving each other an oral at the same time allows you to feed off each other's energy and pleasure as you get closer to the edge of release. This is the perfect position for those who get horny when they see their partner being pleasured and who get turned on by the sound of their partner moaning.

For a twist on this classic when you're feeling adventurous, try flipping the 69 on its back. For the woman, sitting on the man's face can be extremely pleasurable because it puts him in the position to give her great oral while she controls how much pressure she feels. For the man, flipping the 69 on its back leaves your hands free to roam all over her body as you drive her crazy with your oral skills.

The man will lie down on his back as the woman sits on his face. Her body will be facing down on the man's as he starts licking and kissing her clit, maybe even massaging her buttocks as he does. The woman will die down along the man's body, holding herself up with her arms, in the perfect position to begin giving the man an oral at the same time.

With the woman on top, she can adjust her position to her liking to give the man intense fellatio while he stimulates her clit with his tongue and fingers.

93. Flick Move

At the point when she's nearly peeking through oral sex, rapidly give her flick on the clitoris using your tongue. You should ensure the clitoral hood is off the way for a good sensation. Be delicate and make snappy movements with your tongue here and there the clit. Most men commit the error, thinking the clit is simply little nerve finishing in a little area in her body. By doing the oral flick you covering more zone of her and make vibrations that convey the sensation past the reach of your tongue

94. The Edging

This position is an all-get to go to the vulva. The one who receives will lay level on their back with their butt directly at the edge of the bed/counter/lounge chair. The provider stoops (or stands, contingent upon stature) on the floor facing their vulva.

The provider can stick a pad under their knees for additional cushioning. In the event that you need, the one who receives can put their feet on the provider's shoulders for balance, or they can allow dangling their legs. This position opens up the provider's hands for tongue sex, nipple stimulation, or penetration.

95. Saddle Straddle

If your partner is dominant, they are going to love straddling you while you suck and stroke their penis. You can use both your hands and twist up and down their penis while licking around the head.

96. Swiper

Ask your partner to create some suction on your clit by putting their mouth over your labia and clit. Now ask them to shake their heads in circles, side to side, and change up from slow and fast. This will mimic the way many of us masturbate. You can place your bottom on some pillows to give them better access.

97. Deep-Sea Diver

This is another rim job position. This one can be introduced in a shower. If you are new at this, the receiver will remain standing while the giver squats behind them. If you do this in the shower, you won't have to worry about them not being clean.

98. Shark Fin

Because oral sex can't be done underwater, the woman needs to lay down with her hips at the edge of the tub. She will open your legs but keep your feet in the water and enjoy everything your partner is doing to you.

99. Butterball

This position is great for oral but for rim jobs, too. Make sure whoever is receiving, is showered and fresh. They will lie down with their knees pulled up to their chests. This still allows the "doer" to reach the clitoris and breasts of the "receiver." If the male is the receiver, the woman can play will his butt, testicles, and penis. If you don't have dental dams close by, you could grab a sandwich bag or plastic wrap.

Chapter 10.   Orgasm   without Penetration

Best Positions and Tips

100. The Modified Handjob

The modified handjob requires the use of two hands instead of just one. The penis is handled in the normal handjob position while the other hand assists in stroking the shaft or stimulating the balls.

101. The Two in the Pink, One in the Stink

As you may have already noticed, there are a lot of vulgar names associated with sexual acts. This position is definitely one of them. The term "two in the pink, one in the stink" refers to the insertion of two fingers into the vaginal entrance and a single finger into the anal orifice.
The usual fingers used in this position are the index and middle finger for the vagina and the little finger (or pinky) for the anus.

102. Dry Humping

This sexual act is very popular with young adults as they first explore their sexuality. Dry humping allows for all the motions of sex without actual penetration. There is instead a lot of pressure on the pelvic regions as the woman presses her vagina or pubic mound into the penis or any other relatively hard region on the man's body.

103. Penile Rub

This is a different variation of the dry hump without actual penetration. For this act, the man and the woman have their genitals exposed to one another and are actually in close proximity to one another. Using his penis as a tool, the man takes his manhood in his hand and stimulates the woman's clitoris by rubbing the hand against her organ. This can be a precursor to actual sex but has been used as a sexual position for couples who want to achieve orgasm without actual penetration.

104. Breastfucking

This position is included in the tactile category as there is no actual penetration happening during this act.

Basically, the woman squeezes her breasts together to form a cavity which the penis can "penetrate." This act may require proper lubrication as the lack of it can result in chafing of the skin.

Further stimulation can be achieved by allowing the penis to enter into the woman's mouth as the man "thrusts in." Since this act requires the use of the mammaries, it is only logical that the bigger the woman's breasts are, the better the act is performed.

105. Fake Deep Throat

You can get the feeling of deep throating without all the gagging by putting some lube on your hand and using it on the part of his penis that won't go in your mouth. Move your hand in the same motions as your mouth. Look into your partner's eyes to make the connection more intense.

Chapter 11.   Anal Sex

Anal Tips for Beginners

Lubricate

Unlike the vagina, the anus does not lubricate itself naturally. Therefore, you have to use lubricant. There are many on the market that are warming, as well as some that are actually intended to help relax the muscles and make anal a more enjoyable experience for the lady. You should opt for a water-based lubricant of your choice.

Relax

As the lady, you really want to make sure you relax your muscles and take deep breaths. Go slow and take care not to tense up out of fear. In order to help reduce tensing up due to fear, make sure you follow the next step carefully.

Start Small

Especially if you are brand new to anal, as in an anal virgin, you will want to start very small. Using plenty of lube, and a small toy or his pinky finger, he can gently work his way into your bum and help you relax the muscles. He should move slowly and at your discretion, to ensure you are prepared for every step.

Go Slow

Aside from working your way up slowly, all movements should be slow as well. Once you're used to it, and have more confidence in the experience, you can start going faster. But every single anal experience should start with slow movements and shallow penetration. From there, he can choose how deep and quick he will go, based on how she feels.

Communicate

This is the one time you especially want to communicate well during sex. The lady should always be telling the gentleman if what he is doing is okay, and he should not be doing anything she doesn't like or that hurts her. You can even enforce a safe word that means you stop completely if one party is not enjoying themselves or is hurt by it.

Use Additional Stimulation

Anal feels a lot better for a lady if she is being stimulated beyond just through the butt. Rubbing her clitoris and nibbling on her upper shoulders or neck can greatly enhance her experience. As well, having her focus on a pleasurable stimulation taking place elsewhere on her body can help her further relax her muscles and enjoy the experience.

Don't Go from Butt to Vagina

Never go from butt to vagina. Whether it is a finger, his penis, or a toy, nothing should ever penetrate the anus and then the vagina. This can lead to infections that are not enjoyable for anyone.

If You Absolutely Hate It, Stop

The first time or two can be extremely not enjoyable for the female, but eventually it can start feeling better. However, that being said, it should be noticeably better with each experience. If it is clearly not getting better, or it is getting worse, and one or both aren't enjoying it, then stop. You don't need to do it just because! Sex should always be fun and pleasurable for both lovers involved.

Anal Sex Position for First Time

106. The Rear Entry

This is by far a popular choice for too many couples. It is like spooning but on the belly. The girl will need to lie down on her stomach and she can spread her legs apart to give her man the ample amount of room to penetrate her.

The man needs to lie right on the top of his partner and face the same direction. After sufficient lubrication, he can then push his penis inside and give you the pleasure you have been seeking.

107. High Chair

The woman needs to sit on a chair so that the butt must stick out of it. The guy then needs to stand behind. He could kneel down or even squat based on the elevation of the chair. The man would grab his partner's waist and slowly push his penis in the anus. The in and out moment is sure to feel like a rocking chair and will drive both of you crazy with the passion.

Benefits: This is one of the powerful anal sex positions which is likely to give you both a lot of thrill.

108. The Burning Man

The position is simple but you would need a tabletop or even a sofa. The woman needs to lean on the top of sofa or the table and bed so that her anal end is thrusting out. The man then spoons you from behind and after enjoying some oral sex, he pushes his cock inside your hole. It is important to ensure that your table or sofa is such that it doesn't hurt you when leaning on it. Keeping a pillow or blanket might be a good alternative.

Benefits: This form of sex has the potential to get rough as your man could do all he wishes since you are bent on the table and can only moan and shriek in pleasure and pain.

Best Anal Sex Positions

109. The Curled Angel

This sex move is a variation of the sexy spoons position. It allows for intimate closeness, and gives both parties the ability to control the speed and depth of penetration. It works by having the lady laying on whichever side is most comfortable for her. She should have her knees pulled up towards her chest, exposing her bottom to him. The gentleman can then slide in behind her, holding her with his arms, and tuck his legs up under hers. From there, he can penetrate her, and they can work together to control the penetration and intimacy involved in this position.

110. Double Decker

This is a woman on top position that actually gives the man a little more control, but keeps the majority of it with the woman. It is a wonderful position for those who are a little more experienced with anal, or who are good with balance, as slipping could lead to a potentially painful accident. To do it, have the gentleman lay on his back on the bed. He can have his legs outstretched in whatever position is comfortable for him. The lady can then lay on her back over top of him, then prop herself up with her elbows and feet. From there, he can help guide her on to his penis and control the penetration, while she controls the speed and depth at which he enters.

111. Rocking Horse

This is an intimate woman on top position that allows both lovers to engage in a sensual make out session at the same time. It works by having the gentleman sitting up, then leaning back on his hands. His knees can either be bent up to create a seat for her, or his legs can be stretched out to give her free space. Then, the lady can straddle over top of him with a leg on either side of his waist, and guide his penis to penetrate her from behind.

Tips: she can proceed to control the depth, speed and rhythm,

Benefits: Both lovers enjoy a deep and loving gaze, or a sexy make out session.

112. Glowing Triangle

This intimate face to face position is one of the best for anal sex. It is a man on top position that allows for deep penetration, but due to the angle it can inadvertently cause g-spot stimulation at the same time. Ideally, you should have a pillow involved to make this a more comfortable position. To get into form, start by having the lady lay on her back with the cushion under the small of her back holding her bum up in the air. Her knees should be bent with her feet firmly on the bed, helping hold her up and exposed. The gentleman can then slide in between her legs and penetrate her, while she hugs him. For added stimulation, she can use a free hand to rub her clitoris. This is a very sensual position for anal sex that is excellent for a romantic anal experience.

113. Reclining Lotus

This is basically an expansion of the Glowing Triangle, but allows for even more g-spot stimulation through deep penetration. It starts by having the lady laying on her back. Using a pillow under the small of her back helps her expose her anus to the gentleman, so it is ideal to have one handy for this position. Then, she should bend her knees up towards her chest, while letting her legs spread out sideways. The gentleman can then slide up in between her legs and penetrate her bum while keeping his face close to hers. She can either hook her feet under his thighs, or lock her legs behind his back. It is a wonderful position for nuzzling each other or having a steamy make out session while having sex.

114. Afternoon Delight

This is a fun variation of a spooning position that allows for deep penetration while giving the man the majority of the control. It is a very relaxed position that allows you to lovingly gaze into each other's eyes, or simply enjoy the moment. It starts by having the gentleman laying on whatever side is more comfortable for him, with his knees slightly bent for balance. Then, the lady lays on her back on a 90-degree angle from him, with her bum lined up to his penis. He can then penetrate her and thrust at whatever speed and depth is comfortable for the both of them.

115. The Amazon

This is a lady on top position that requires a chair or a stool to be done. It can be a very sensual move that allows for nuzzling and romancing while engaging in some delightful anal sex. To start, the gentleman should sit comfortably on a seat that has no arms. Then, the lady can mount him, while facing him, and having a leg on either side. She can continue to control the thrusting for whatever is most comfortable for her. Either the gentleman or the lady can use a spare hand to stimulate her clitoris or breasts (or both!) to add to the pleasure of this move.

116. The Basket

This position is a lady on top move that allows for both parties to have almost equal control over the movements. The basket allows for both lovers to face one another, and have a free hand for additional stimulation to enhance the move. To start, the gentleman should sit on a comfortable surface with his legs out straight. He should be sitting up enough that he doesn't have to use his hands to support himself. Then, the lady can straddle him with a leg on either side of his waist, while controlling the penetration. She can use his shoulders for leverage, while he puts his hands under her bum to help lift her up and down on his penis. This move allows for you to move as slowly or as quickly as you desire.

Chapter 12.   Sex Positions to Keep Her Coming

Multiple Female Orgasms

There are two different types of multiple orgasms that a woman can have. The first is called a Blended Orgasm, and the second is Subsequent Orgasms.

Blended Orgasms

A blended orgasm occurs when two or more different erogenous zones are being stimulated at the same time. In this part, we will talk about the intense double orgasm that can occur when both the clitoris and the G-Spot are being stimulated, as well as other types of blended orgasms that can be achieved.

If both her G-Spot and her clitoris are being stimulated at the same time and both are being done in a way that is bringing her intense pleasure, she may be able to orgasm through both methods at the same time. Since there are multiple different types of orgasms that women are able to achieve, these different orgasms can happen simultaneously for double or triple the pleasure! When a woman is aroused, there is an increase in blood flow to the areas which are stimulated. When the clitoris is being stimulated, there is increased blood flow to the clitoris, and the same thing happens when the G-Spot is stimulated. If the nipples are being stimulated, there is an increase in blood flow there as well. This causes arousal at the site of stimulation. When a blended orgasm occurs, the areas being pleasured both have increased blood flow at the same time and this makes for two distinct orgasms, which compound to give her a mind-blowing full-body orgasm, especially if the two locations are more separate from each other- like the nipples and the clitoris.

Subsequent Orgasms

Not only can women have blended orgasms, but they can also have back-to-back orgasms. These orgasms occur one after the other and give the woman immense pleasure because she is able to keep coming again and again and again.

This type of repeated orgasm is only possible for women, as the male's penis is unable to do this. This is due to the fact that the male body has to wait for a refractory period after every orgasm. What this means is that there is an amount of time after an orgasm during which a man's body is unable to achieve an erection or have another orgasm. During this time, his body is recovering from the orgasm and needs this time to recuperate. The length of this period is different for every man, but it ranges between fifteen to thirty minutes in most males. The great thing about the clitoris is that after orgasm, it may be very sensitive for a few minutes, but it maintains its "erection" and can be stimulated again a very short time after for a doubly-pleasurable second orgasm. This can lead to a third and a fourth and beyond

Best Kama Sutra Positions

117. The Seashell

Lay back on the bed with your feet raised all the way up and your ankles crossed behind your head. Now he can get into the missionary position and thrust back and forth.

Benefits: Before trying this, you may want to stretch a little! This will really hit your G-spot and your hands will be free to stimulate your clitoris.

118. The Cat

The man lies on top of the woman as if in the missionary position and enters the woman. He then moves his body up the woman slowly until he can't get any higher without hurting himself. Instead of thrusting he will grind in small circles. This will stimulate the clitoris as the base of the penis rubs against it.

Benefit: This is particularly good for woman who don't normally come by penetration on its own. It is almost guaranteed to give a woman a deep satisfying orgasm.

119. Closed for Business

This is another oral sex position for your man going down on you. Probably the simplest out of them all, you lay on your back with your legs closed together!

Benefits: This position works great if you sometimes find that direct clitoral stimulation is too much. Pull up your pubic area whilst he does this to feel the full sensation.

120. Bridge

Begin by having your man lay across two objects (bed and chair) leaving his mid-section un-suspended acting as a 'bridge' between the two. Start by sitting on him from the side then slowly bring your leg over so you are now facing away from him. Keep thrusting a few times in between turns.

Benefits: You are in control of everything whilst giving him an amazing corkscrew sensation.

121. Dinner is Served

Begin by wrapping your legs around your partners waist and have him hold your bum and back like he is carrying you. Have him penetrate you in this position then slowly lean back so your back is parallel to the floor. Your partner should find it easiest to hold you by placing his hands midway up your back.

Benefits: This one is really good fun to try and just getting into the position can result it lots of laughter. To carry this off properly your partner must have good upper body strength.

122. Ballet Dancer

This position can be tiring on the legs for both partners. First you must stand on a hard surface close to something that you can hold should you need support. Take a step forward with one leg and lower your pelvis closer to the ground like a lunge. Have your man do the same, have him lunge lower close to you so he can penetrate you. Now by either partner going deeper or higher in the lunge, this can create an intense orgasm.

Benefits: Both partners are able to control the speed at which they go and they can control how deep the penetration is. This can be tricky as you must remain balance throughout.

123. Leg Up

You stand facing one another. She raises one of her legs up and wraps it around your waist or thigh and squeezes to pull you in closer.

Benefits: No furniture is required so this position is great for spontaneous sex where you don't have access to a bedroom.

124. Dirty Dancing

This position can be done almost anywhere and if you need more support it can be done on a desk or hard surface. The man needs to lean on a wall facing the woman whilst holding her. The woman straddles her man and one leg is wrapped around his waist for balance. Now both of you are able to rock together rather than just your partner thrusting

Benefits: This position will feel great for both man and woman. He will have great access to your boobs and intimacy is created due to the proximity of your bodies. In this position you are able to control how deep he penetrates and how much clitoral stimulation you receive.

125. Back Breaker

Lie on the bed with your legs hanging off the edge, shift your bum forward until that is also off the end. Your man will kneel in front of you and penetrate you. No push up onto your toes and arch your back. Get your man to hold your bum and then he can begin to thrust.

Benefits: This position is great when you are focusing on your man however pushing onto your toes can heighten your orgasm. In this position it is very easy to hit the G-spot just by slightly changing the arch in your back.

126. Pretzel Dip

Start by laying on your side, have your partner straddle your leg that is resting on the bed. Bring your other leg around the front and wrap it around his waist.

Benefits: This position gives really deep penetration and your partner will have his hands free to feel your boobs or clitoris

127. Butter Churner

Start by laying on your back and bringing your feet over your head so that your bum is pointing up in the air. Have your man stand over you ad squat up and down entering you each time he does.

Benefits: Each time he squats it will be like he is entering you for the first time over and over again.

128. The Landslide

Start by laying on your stomach. Prop yourself onto your forearms and have your legs slightly apart. Have your partner sit just behind your bum with his legs both side and hands behind him leaning onto them. He can now penetrate you and begin rocking back and forth.

Benefits: It can really hit your G-spot and by bringing your legs closer together your man will feel fuller inside you.

129. The Thigh Master

This position is very similar to reverse cowgirl so begin in that position, woman on top facing away from your partner. Have your man bring up his knees so you can lean onto them for support.

Benefits: Being on top is great for the female orgasm whichever way you do it, by your partner having his knees up he will feel fuller inside you.

130. The Hinge

Have your partner kneel up on the bed and lean back supporting his weight with one hand. Position yourself facing away from him in the doggy position. Place your thighs either side of him and lean onto your elbows, now move backwards until he has entered you.

Benefits: You are able to control the depth of penetration and speed.

131. High Dive

This position can be carried out anyway horizontal, through experimentation you will find where best suits you however a hard surface such as the floor is suggested. Begin by straddling your partner, woman on top style, begin by having sex in this position. Balance your hands either side of your man so you can gradually ease your legs out straight over his. By hooking your feet around his this will keep your legs secure. With your hands either side of his chest, get him to put his hands under yours to take some of your weight whilst you both bring your hands in to your elbows. Now lift your chest and stomach up off him and begin moving up and down.

Benefits: This position can create intimacy as you can look into each other's eyes. He will also have a great view of your breasts. This may be difficult to master as your arms can get tired easily, however the orgasm that can be achieved in this position can be extremely powerful.

132. Shoulder Stand

You will begin by laying on your back with your partner kneeling in front of you. Wrap your legs around him and allow him to lift you up so he is able to enter you. He will support you with one hand holding up your back whilst you shift your body weight onto your shoulders. Whilst still holding you he can now thrust in and out of you.

Benefits: This is a great position for you as it allows extremely deep penetration and amazing orgasms. If you arch your back slightly you are more likely to hit your G-spot. Be aware that as he is holding some of your weight he may get tired faster.

133. Erotic V

Begin by sitting down on the edge of a table or desk. Have your partner stand in front of you and crouch down slightly so he can enter you. Put your arms around his neck and slowly pull one leg up at a time onto your partner's shoulders.

Benefits: You are both able to look at each other whilst doing it making it much more intimate. Lean back and have your partner hold your bum for more support.

134. Catherine Wheel

The man and woman begin by sitting facing each other. You must shuffle forward until you can wrap your legs around his torso. The man can now enter you, have him wrap one leg over you to hold you in place. To make the position steadier have him hold his weight on his elbow and you must hold your weight leaning back onto your hands.

Benefits: Great for slow, passionate sex. Often results in simultaneous orgasm.

135. On Your Mark

Start by laying on your back on a chair with both legs straight up in the air. Your partner gets on his hands and knees with his behind facing you. It can be tricky to penetrate so you may find it easier for your partner to be on his feet with his hands on the floor to balance him.

Benefits: This position requires a certain amount of athleticism, it may not feel as good as other positions but certainly is fun.

136. The Seated Ball

The woman starts by crouching low on a bed. Her partner can enter her by moving closer in a seated position. She can then control the movement by rocking backwards and forwards.

Benefits: You will be controlling the movement and speed at which things happen. Your partner can also kiss your back and neck which can feel great with his penis inside you.

137. Kentucky Derby

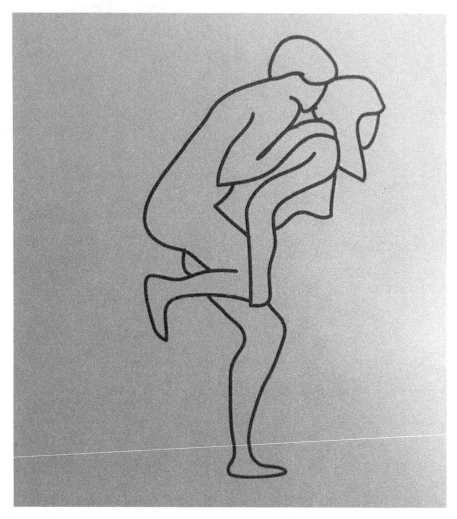

This is basically a piggy back ride sex position. Have your man jump onto your back as if you are giving him a piggy back. Have him enter you from behind and gently thrust.

Benefits: Similar to some other sex positions this can give a lot of laughs when trying to get into the position. You must be strong enough to hold your partners weight so this may not be suitable if your partner is a lot bigger than you.

138. Hovering Butterfly

Begin by laying on your back on a hard piece of furniture. Have your man stand in front of you and place your legs over his shoulders. Have your hands lift up your bum and hips. Have your man hold your bum to help support you.

Benefits: Great for you as you do not have to do any work. The angle of your pelvic area will provide extremely deep penetration, really hitting your G-spot.

139. The G-Spot Sniper

The woman lies on her back and extends her legs. The man kneels down right in front of her, in between her legs. He grabs her hips and pulls her closer to him while lifting her hips off the bed. She lifts her legs straight up in the air, pointing towards the ceiling. He then guides his penis and enters her. He only inserts the head of his penis, which is shallow penetration. This is to make sure that the expanded and sensitive penis head directly rubs only at the sensitive G spot.

Why: The head of the penis is directly rubbing against the G spot, as the name of this sex position suggests. By concentrating on this sensitive spot, the woman can reach her climax. In addition, because of the limited thrusting and penetration, the man can last longer before he, too reaches his climax.

Chapter 13.   Menstrual   Cycle   and Sex

Menstrual Cycle Basics

During a woman's younger years, she will get her period every month. Period is the casual term for menstruation, and it is how it will be referred to hereafter. Once a month, if a woman does not get pregnant, she will get her period, which involves the lining of her uterus being shed. This makes way for the possibility of pregnancy the next month, as the uterus will develop a new lignin over the month. A period usually lasts about a week and involves skin cells and blood being shed through the vagina. The reason for this is that there is extra skin and blood that accumulate in the uterus to prepare for a possible pregnancy, but it will only last for one month at a time.

Benefits and How it Affects Sex

If a woman is comfortable, there is no problem with her having sex during her period. There is nothing that says that a woman should not, and it will not hurt the man or the woman. As long as neither of them is afraid of blood, the only difference will be the mess that it will cause. Women actually tend to have a much higher sex drive during their periods and during the week leading up to it.

There are some benefits that come from having sex on your period. One of these benefits is that having sex while on your period can actually offer relief from the pain of period cramps. Period cramps can be very painful, and anything that makes them feel better is a welcome suggestion, especially when it feels as good as sex will. This result is because of the orgasm. The chemicals that are released in the brain make you feel happy and also have pain relief functions. The other reason is that an orgasm makes the uterus contract and then release. The release part of this will likely make a woman feel better than she did before in terms of cramps.

Another benefit of having an orgasm during your period is that it leads to the uterus contracting, which actually pushes the blood and uterus contents out faster, leading to a shorter period length. This also means that there is ample natural lubrication and that lubricant is not necessary during period sex.

Best Kama Sutra Positions to Try During Menstruation

A good way to have sex during menstruation is in the shower. This makes it so that there is not much cleanup involved, and the blood that gets on either of you will be able to be washed off right away. This is a cleaner and more comfortable alternative to having sex in bed and having to jump in the shower afterward. Additionally, shower sex is steamy (literally) and hot (literally) and can make for some very fun body-on-body action. Make sure the water is the perfect temperature and that you have a mat or something on the floor so you aren't slipping all over the place! Before you start any type of penetration in the water, make sure you use lots of waterproof lube because the water in the shower won't be enough of a lubricant for the inside of a vagina and will actually make for some painful friction. Let's avoid that; lube is your friend!

140. Standing Doggy Style

Standing Doggy Style is a position from the Kama Sutra with a twist. It is a good place to start with shower sex because it will make sure that you don't get sprayed in the face with a hot stream of water while you are trying to focus on having a blissful orgasm. Pleasurable for both parties, Doggy Style in the shower is a new take on an old favorite.

The man stands with his back to the running water with the woman standing in front of him, facing away from him. The woman then bends forward and can put her hands on the edge of the tub or the wall of the shower for support. The man slides his penis into her from behind, grabbing onto her hips for a deeper thrust, and then they are ready to go for it. This position has a good chance of the man being able to hit the woman's G-spot with his penis, so this position will be greatly enjoyed by the woman. The warmth and the wet environment of the shower are sure to make for an unforgettable sexual encounter.

141. Kama Sutra Shower Sex Position

This is another position to try in the shower. If you both are in the mood for a position that doesn't need you to focus too much on difficult positioning and holding yourselves up in a slippery shower, you can try the kneeling position. Have yourselves kneel on the floor of the shower, one person behind the other? From here, you can go in many different ways. You can use this position as foreplay as you both reach around to pleasure the other's genitals with your hands before you move to the bedroom together. You can also use this as foreplay before switching to another position for penetration in the shower. Or you can start penetration right away. For penetration, you will have to adjust each of your heights on your knees to line up your erection and her vagina to meet nicely for smooth penetration. This position is full of possibilities and is a very hot way to get you both in the mood for whatever is to come either in the shower or out of it.

142. Bouncy Chair

This is not a shower position, but it is a great position for having sex during your period. This is because it can be done on the floor so that you can more easily clean up afterward.

To get into this position, the man will get on his knees on the floor (on towels or sheets for ease of cleaning) and sit back on his heels. The woman will sit on his lap, facing him, and put his penis inside of her. She will keep her feet planted on the floor and use the balls of her feet to bounce herself up and down on the man's penis. This position is great because the woman is hovering over the floor and this will allow for most of the blood to land there instead of all over the bed or the man.

Things to Keep in Mind

There are a few things to keep in mind if you and your partner decide that you wish to have sex on your period.

1. Blood Stains

Ensure that before you begin, if you are going to have sex anywhere outside of the bathtub or the shower, that you put down a lot of towels or something that will be able to absorb the blood. If you get it on your white bed sheets, it will stain. Keep I mind as well that whatever towels you choose to lay down will also likely be stained, so be sure to choose those that you don't need to keep freshly white.

2. Self-Consciousness

Having sex during her period may make a woman feel self-conscious. Keeping this in mind is important as she may feel sensitive about her body or the amount of blood that is involved.

3. Sexually Transmitted Infections

One thing that is important to note is that there are some STIs that are transmitted through the blood. These are HIV or hepatitis. In order to stay safe, it is important to use condoms all the time, but especially when there will be blood involved during sex.

4. Tampons

Tampons that are forgotten about when having sex can cause a problem. If you were wearing a tampon before having sex, ensure that you remove it before a penis or fingers are inserted into the vagina. Otherwise, the tampon will need to be removed by a doctor.

5. You Can Still Get Pregnant

While the chances are lower during your period, you can still become impregnated during your period. It is difficult to say at what point your body will be ready to conceive during your period, so taking adequate precautions is necessary.

Chapter 14.   Sexual Fantasies

A sexual fantasy is something that a person imagines or dreams of doing or taking part in, in a sexual context. This fantasy is something that, when imagined, leads the person to become sexually aroused. A sexual fantasy will commonly involve something that you would not regularly have the chance to do. For example, it could be something like having sex with a jail guard as their inmate. In this case, this is not something that you would likely do, but you fantasize about doing it as it arouses you.

Common Sexual Fantasies

Sexual fantasies often come in the form of role play. Like the example above, a sexual fantasy often needs to be acted out, such as one person playing the role of the jail guard and the other playing the part of the inmate. This is a common sexual fantasy, and this brings us to the first category of sexual fantasies.

Power Dynamic Fantasies

Many fantasies and role plays involve some type of power dynamic, where one person has control over the other or is in an authoritative role, while their partner is submissive to them.

Kink

Another common type of sexual fantasy involves kink. This can include things like restricted movement from being tied up, being spanked or spanking their partner, or having sex wearing specific things like leather or fur.

194

Fetishes

The final category that we will look at involves fetishes. This can be something like fantasizing about having someone suck on your toes, fantasizing about peeing on someone or having them pee on you, wishing to have sex in a large group, or wanting to have sex with a mask on.

As I'm sure you can see, the different categories of sexual fantasies involve a lot of overlap, which. Is why they are most often referred to as the general umbrella of "sexual fantasies?"

  Best Sexual Fantasies for Beginners Who Want to Try New Things

Now that you understand sexual fantasies, I am going to share some common sexual fantasies that are great for beginners who are looking to spice up their sex life a little bit.

The Photo Shoot

The first example of a sexual fantasy comes in the form of a role play. This role play is The Photo Shoot role play. In this role play, one person will play the model, and one person will play the photographer. You can begin acting out how a regular photoshoot would go, with one person posing for photos clothed in front of the camera. The photographer can tell the model what poses they want to see. As it progresses, the photographer can tell the model to take off some items of clothing, or the model can do this on their own. As they take more layers of clothing off, the photographer can ask them to do more and more sensual positions for the camera. Eventually, the photographer can go in to help them get undressed, or when they are fully naked, the photographer can step in to help the model move their body into poses they want to see. With the touch barrier broken, they can then continue to touch each other. The model can position themselves in positions with their legs spread, their but out their breasts towards the camera, anything. This will eventually progress to the photographer touching the model, and sex ensues.

Public Sex

Some sexual fantasies involve having sex in new or nerve-wracking locations. One example of this is public sex. This can involve having sex in a movie theatre, in an alleyway, in a boardroom of the office, and so on. Maybe you fantasize about this while having sex at home in your bedroom, or maybe you take it to the actual place that you fantasize about and try it for real!

Handcuffs/Tying Up

Handcuffs are a sexy and simple introduction to the world of restraint and domination that you have probably heard of before. This is a great place to start because the person being restricted can still express their desires and wishes for pleasure, but the other person is ultimately in charge of what they choose to agree to and what they do not. Because both partners can still see and talk to each other, they can communicate throughout, telling the other person how to touch them and what they like. The fact that one partner is in control will be the thing that makes both of you go wild with desire.

Chapter 15. Best Sex Positions Not In The Bed

143. The Waterfall

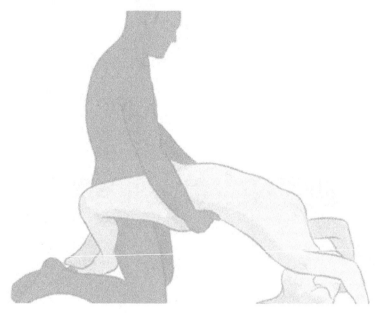

The male should find a secure chair and sit on it. The female can position herself facing towards the male with her legs either side of him. The female should then lower herself on to his penis for penetration. Once inserted, the male should use his hands to support the female behind her back and bottom. The female should then slowly lean backwards until her head is on the floor. While performing, the male should take care to support the female's weight. However, the female should take care to move slowly to ensure that the male is not experiencing any strain or discomfort.

Tips: This position requires penile flexibility, else there is a risk of the male straining his suspensor ligaments! If you want to find out if the male's penis is flexible enough, have him stand against a wall. Pull his penis gradually down. If the penis can point directly down to the ground without causing pain then you should be fine to perform this position, but still be careful.

The female should stay still when the male is initially penetrating her and guide the penis to the vagina. The female should wait while he finds the most comfortable position and angle to thrust without injury.

A pillow should also be used on the floor to comfort the female's head during sex. The male should sit in a sturdy chair. The female can then climb on top with her legs either side of him. She should lean back until her head is on the floor.

Benefits: The clitoris is very accessible in this position so is great for stimulation during sex. There is also a lot of friction inside the vagina so this is great all-rounder for reaching orgasm.

144. The Eagle

The eagle position has the female on her back with her legs spread open while the male inserts himself inside her from the front. He will grab her thighs and continue to thrust into her while her legs are spread open, giving him an amazing view of penetration, her clitoris and her breasts and face during intercourse. She also has the freedom to stimulate her clitoris if necessary to achieve climax.

145. The Sphinx

An interesting rendition of the highly popular, doggy style position, the sphinx involved the woman laying on her stomach, sitting up on her elbows. She will then pull one leg up to her side and leave another leg stretched. The male will then put his weight on his hands, leaning over her with his legs stretched behind him, inserting himself inside her. He will then move up and down, thrusting gently.

Tips: She can also help take some of the strain off of him but bouncing back onto him instead of having him do all the work.

146. The Column

This position involved both parties standing up, the male behind the female. The male will then insert himself inside her from behind, wrapping his hands around her waist and placing them on her pubic region.

Tips: She can place her hands over his or on a surface in front of her.

Benefits: The position is great for a couple who wants to have a quickie.

147. The Good Spread

To start, the gentleman should be lying on his back with his legs however he feels are most comfortable. Then, the lady should mount him, facing him, but sitting upright. Each leg should be stretched out on either side of him, and she can lean forward slightly and use his chest to help her bounce up and down on him. Take care not to bounce out of control, as that could hurt him. Then, he can admire her while she pleasures herself on him.

Tips: This position is best if the lady is flexible, as it requires her to have her legs stretched out straight to either side. The man will have free hands, so he can rub her thighs or massage her breasts while she rides him.

Benefits: It allows for deep penetration, and for the woman to control the speed and rhythm, as well as where she is being stimulated by him.

148. The Melody Maker

To start, have the female lay back over a piece of furniture, with her feet firmly on the floor. Then, he can come in between her legs and penetrate her.

Tips: Depending on the height of the furniture, he may or may not have to get down on his knees to be at the same height as her. He can hold her hands, stimulate her clitoris, massage her breasts, or do anything they desire.

Benefits: This position takes control away from the female entirely and gives it to the male. It is perfect for hitting the g-spot, and gives the gentleman the ability to use his spare hand to stimulate her clitoris at the same time, ensuring she will achieve a mind-blowing orgasm. Bonus points if they both orgasm at the same time!

149. Stand and Carry

She starts off lying down, and he will lean over her. She wraps her arms around his neck and her legs around his waist once he enters you. He then wraps his arms around her and brings her to a standing position.

Tips: He can grab her butt to help move her up and down.

Benefits: This is a standing position that does not use a couch, bed, or wall.

Chapter 16. Level Up Hard-Core Sex Positions

150. Free Limbo

In Free limbo, the woman should lean backwards and support herself on the bed using her hands. When positioning herself, she should be careful to be slow enough to ensure that she does not over-strain his man's penis. Once in the perfect position, she has to thrust her body up and down slowly with the aid of her legs. The woman can also be able to grind the man by moving her hips backwards and forwards in relatively slow motion. On the other hand, the man should always make sure that he is comfortable and enjoys himself without any much pressure on his penis. He can decide to hold onto your hips and move them back and forth as you grind him. This sex position is so intimate since it entails both partners facing each other. It is also a very easy style to execute as it has no major complications if it is done in the right way.

151. L train

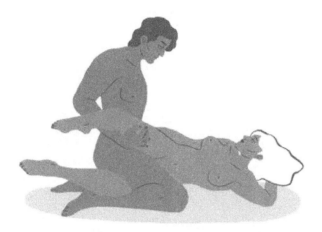

This is basically said in the name. The letter that is made in this position is the letter L. This position is almost similar to the doggy style. There is a difference between the doggy style and this position here since the woman instead of positioning themselves in a dog walking style the woman lies on the side. After the woman has lied on their side then the man goes behind her and kneels. Here he positions himself near the sexual area of the woman who is his partner. The man then positions the woman's leg into an L letter. In this position, the woman is comfortable without having to kneel and bend their backs. This is very uncomfortable for the woman and this position, therefore, makes the woman's work easy. Remember for pleasure to be found there must be a lot of comfortability. So this position has readily provided that. The L position also allows the man to penetrate more than in most sex position, therefore, it is really a good position. It also allows the man to hit the woman's g-spot just like in the doggy style position. If one needs to make the woman sexually satisfied you can always trust that this position. It makes the pleasure for the woman intense and undeniable and the woman will be able to orgasm even if she has never gone through it before.

152. Raised Doggy

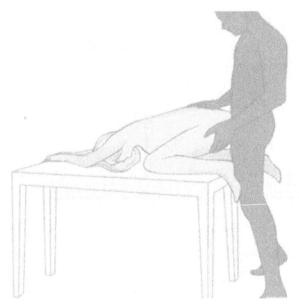

In this position, the woman has the legs and hands on a raised platform and the man standing behind her.

Tips: For those couples with a big height difference, this is among the ideal positions that they can try.

153. Lift off

The position is among one of the intimate anal sex. You will enjoy it when you decide to use a pillow to lift her hips. When she lay on her back, put a pillow under her hips and another one under her head. You have to support your weight with your hands and enter her slowly. Make sure that she will feel it when you enter her and if possible, make her yell a little. The yelling should not be because of pain, but pleasure, she is feeling when you are sliding inside her.

Tips: She can opt to help you do it better by placing her hands on your hips. When she does this, you will be in a position to access the tempo that will make her feel as if she is in another world.

Benefits: It is enjoyable, and you will not regret thinking about it. It is a great idea to play it, and it will create a strong bond between you and her. The sweetness of that spot will make her find the pleasure that she wants.

154. Side Roll

The side to side sex position is another variation of the spooning sex position. This sex position is a favor to individuals who have huge bodies and finds the spooning position complicated for them. In this position, both partners lay side by side facing each other. Depending on the sex type one is having, the positions and approaches taken vary. If you are having anal sex, the woman will have to just lean forward and backwards while either straightening or bending their legs. In this position, the woman can be able to rub themselves to get an orgasm as the man penetrates her when having anal sex.

In the side to side position, the man can easily penetrate the woman slowly and luxuriously. This position is also pleasing to both partners since the woman can be able to caress herself or the man with ease during sex. On the other hand, both partners can even find time to easily kiss while having sex thus get whole pleasure. While penetrating, the man can choose to go slow or fast to allow the partners to have longer intimate experience thus an increased pleasure to both partners. In this position, the partners will also get a good time to strongly bond and strengthen their relationship thus making it so intimate and pleasurable.

This position is ideal for a quick - very quick, in fact - lovemaking session. It requires a great deal of strength, flexibility, and balance on the man's part, and may be best performed on a bed or other soft surface. That way, no one will get hurt if the man needs to come out of the position. To start, the man will create a bridge with his body (also known to yogis as a full-wheel backbend) and the woman will straddle him in this position,

moving herself up and down. To take the weight
she should support herself with her feet while doing
position too long, though - while it's difficult to hold
can also create dizziness for the man from all of the bl
head.

156. Standing Doggy

Standing Doggy Style is a position from the Kama Sutra with a twist. It is
a good place to start with shower sex because it will make sure that you

sprayed in the face with a hot stream of water while you are
trying to focus on having a blissful orgasm. Pleasurable for both parties,
Doggy Style in the shower is a new take on an old favorite.

The man stands with his back to the running water with the woman
standing in front of him, facing away from him. The woman then bends
forward and can put her hands on the edge of the tub or the wall of the
shower for support. The man slides his penis into her from behind,
grabbing onto her hips for a deeper thrust, and then they are ready to go
for it. This position has a good chance of the man being able to hit the
woman's G-spot with his penis, so this position will be greatly enjoyed by
the woman. The warmth and the wet environment of the shower are sure
to make for an unforgettable sexual encounter.

157. The Prayer Pose

The prayer pose will require some flexibility on the man's part. If he has
tight leg muscles, the couple may find this position a bit difficult. Yet, it's
not impossible to master, and it can encourage deep penetration. The
woman, too, will need a fair amount of strength in order to master this.
To begin, the man will lie on his back and draw his knees up towards his
chest. From there, the woman will sit backwards on top of him, with his
legs still drawn up, and slide him inside of her while propping herself up
on his feet. This will require a great deal of balance from both partners.
To make things simpler, both he and she can grab one another's wrists or
forearms for better balance.

158. The Recliner

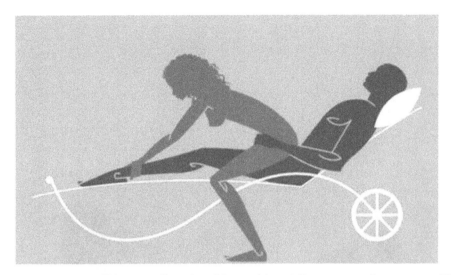

Only the man will be standing for this position. The woman, however, will sit atop a desk or table ledge of appropriate height, and spread her legs. Both legs can be pressed atop the man's shoulders, if the woman is flexible enough to allow for this. Depending on the man's height, he may need to bend his knees slightly to reach the ideal entering position. The woman can lean back to brace herself as he thrusts.

159. Butt lift

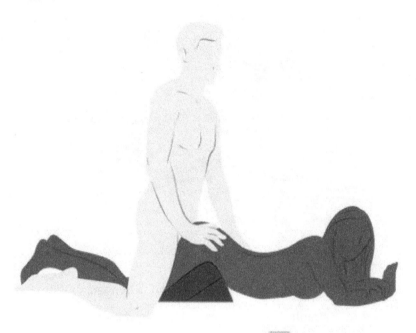

This position requires the woman to lay on her back on a piece of furniture. The edge of the bed is ok, but tables, desks and countertops work better for this because of the stability. The man stands up straight and puts the woman's legs on either shoulder. The woman lifts up her pelvis and the man grabs onto her bottom. One inside of her, he can easily move the woman up and down, depending on his strength. If the woman is heavier or if the man is unable to hold onto the woman, several pillows can be added underneath the small of the woman's back to give her a significant amount of elevation with a lot less effort on the male's part.

This position also allows for deep penetration and gives the man a great view while doing so. The woman can use her free hands to either grasp onto the edge of the surface she is laying on to help take some of the pressure off of the man. If no assistance is needed from the man, the woman can put on a show for the man by grabbing her breasts or twisting and tickling her nipples. She can also rub her clitoris to help with stimulation and achieving orgasm.

160. Frog Style

It's the doggie-style, but instead of being on all fours, the woman lies on her face, with her arms stretched out and her buttocks in the air. Anytime someone's face is positioned down, it's recommended that it be on a bed, not the floor. Many of these positions already have you feeling awkward, if not uncomfortable. Why compound that with carpet burns or marks from a hard wood floor? The cushioning of a mattress or maybe even a pillow might be just the thing to make the position work for the both of you.

The advantage to this is that the woman can last longer without having to support her upper have and she can use her hands that would've otherwise been trembling from supporting top half to pleasure herself. The man has his hands free to, so he can provide stimulation to the breast and back.

161. Flying Buttress

This is a position that is very nice for people who are flexible. This refers to the woman. The people who mostly do this position are either used to doing yoga or even ballerinas. If you are not really flexible this then is not a position you should really take into consideration. So this is the right position to take if you know you can handle a lot of stretching happening on your body. The position that is being discussed allows the man to reach the g-spot which allows the woman to feel pleasure and to finally orgasm. If it is not hit then pleasure is the last thing you are to expect. In this position, the man can easily reach the g-spot of a woman. This position comes to be where the woman can place her legs on top of her head. This is possible when the woman is lying down then the lifting of the legs follow. The man can set the woman's legs on his shoulders to make the woman be totally comfortable during the process. So at the end of it, all this position is great for people who have full-body coordination. The man is in charge when it comes to this position and he is the one who guides the whole process of sex.

162. Howdy Style

To get into this position, the woman should first lie down in the missionary position with her back on the bed and her legs and arms straight. The woman spread her legs wide apart and the man kneels in front to penetrate her. He then holds her ankles to keep her in place as he thrusts into her. He can stimulate her manually with his hands or he can lean forward to use his tongue, and she can also stimulate herself with her hands to give the man a show. The woman can vary her stimulation by changing the angle of her thighs and can prolong her thighs behind raised up by pressing them against his body.

The man is in full control of this position and is able to watch the woman enjoy the act, which is a good visual show. The man can also vary the speed.

Deep penetration is achieved during this act so the woman should be fully aroused and lubricated for this position. In addition, the woman can relax her legs by bringing them down every now and again.

163. Special Breakfast

For the Special breakfast, the woman lies on the table on her back, bends the elbows and uses them to lift the body. The man will sit on a chair between the woman's thighs and puts her legs on his shoulders. He leans forward with his head to touch the woman with his mouth.

164. Fantasy Pose

Here, the woman will lie on a fitness ball on her side with her leg and arm on the floor. The other hand is put on the ball close to the waist in order to balance her body and be able to lift the other leg. The man will kneel in a way that the leg is between the man's thighs. Her other leg is placed on his should. The man will embrace the woman using one hand and use the other hand to grab her thigh.

165. Got YOU!

This is A great little sort of kinky one especially If you are a little into bondage. Simply lay on a surface that is high enough to go to or just below his waist. If that isn't possible do it on the edge of a bed or from the floor but in this case the male will have to be on his knees as far down as he can go. You also may want to put a pillow under her hips to raise her if needed.

Lay the female back completely, you are in front of her facing her and she locks her ankles around the neck of the guy. Commence thrusting away. This also does about the same thing to her Kegal muscles as the position on the ball. This is great for sensation but be aware that you have to gauge with your partner how much power to put behind those hips.

166. Got YOU Two!

This is the opposing position for nineteen! We have to be fair now. This one is a bit more daunting than the other because you are being held in blissful hostage by your own legs. Now, for this we suggest a lot of stretching and a little Yoga maybe prior to attempting this one.

Lay the female on her back on a surface that is at the male hip level. If the bed is high enough then you can do well there and if not then the floor, again with pillow under hips to elevate if needed. This is actually a great

223

position for sensation if you prefer a more back stimulation in the vagina rather than front.

167. Surrender

This position is a nifty one of course it's all on the female here but if you are an eager little devil and you want to be able to really enjoy the top position. This would be where the male is on his back hanging off the bed or big soft chair.

Not recommended with say a kitchen chair variety. This would hurt the upper back and be kind of dangerous.

As he lays back his penis and hips will be thrust up in such a way that will be more beneficial to both but certainly the female. The female of course can bounce or use the vertical slide method that we have described in appropriate exercises.

168. Side Slide

This position can be started in the position nine pose. The difference is to make sure he is sitting up with the main focus being him pressed as far into the female as possible. The female's legs would be pointed up to the ceiling and the male is holding one knee over his shoulder while he is leaned to the side closest to that leg.

This is very effectual with a great feel for both parties. The last several poses we described leads to the deepest pressure inside the female.

169. Book Ends Position

Both will begin on their knees facing each other. He will spread his knees so that he can be closer to the bed while she will remain tall. Once he has lowered himself so that he is in line with her, he can slip his penis inside.

Tips: If comfortable, he can move his knees back together.

170. Big Dipper

This is a tiring sex position, so don't plan on being here too long. You will need a sturdy chair that faces your sofa or bed.

- He will position himself so that he isn't quite sitting in the chair, with his hands resting on the chair and his feet on the bed or sofa. He will be completely elevated off the ground. He will look like he is going to do a tricep dip.

- She will then straddle him as she is facing him, but she should not place any weight on him.

- He will then lower himself and push back up, moving in and out of her.

171. The Yab-Yum Position

Get together in the Yab-Yum position. A staple position in Tantric sex and the position that everything begins from. The man sits down with his legs crossed. The woman sits on his lap, her legs wrapped around him. You can do this position at the headboard of your bed so that one of you can lean on it for support if need be. Getting together like this brings you close at every point of your body, from your eyes to your chest to your feet. From here, we can begin to connect deeper than ever before. Synchronize your breathing with each other. You can look into each other's eyes if you wish. Sync up the speed and depth of your breathing and make sure it's not too shallow or too quick. Relax into this with each other and let your feelings guide you. You can do this for some time and let the experience unfold. Try to get in tune with the feelings of your body and see if you are receiving anything from the other person in their energy or their breath.

172. Rock-A-Bye Booty

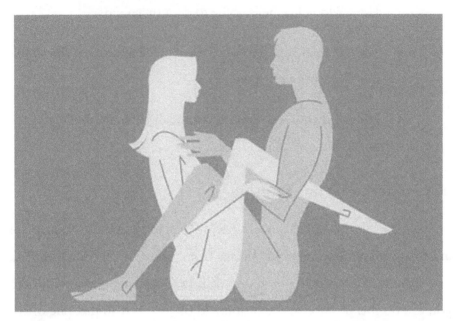

This one can be a bit tricky for people who aren't exactly flexible.

Start with the man on his back, and the lady slowly straddles him. Once he is in her, he will lift his torso, and she will position herself so that they are face-to-face. Both will wrap their legs tightly around each other's buttocks. Both will link elbows under the other's knees and bring them up so that they are at chest level.

Tips: This position will require a rocking motion since thrusting isn't possible in this position. The woman can squeeze her pelvic floor muscles to provide him with a stronger sensation.

173. Torrid Tidal Wave

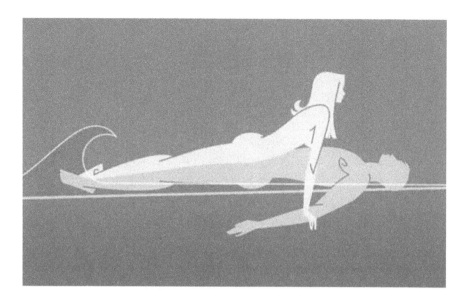

He will lie on his back, keeping his legs together. She will straddle his penis and then move to lay stretched out on top of him, pelvises aligned. She will lift up her torso so that she is resting on her hands. The slightest movements will provide pleasing friction.

Tips: This is great for an intense make-out session.

174. The Sofa Spread-Eagle

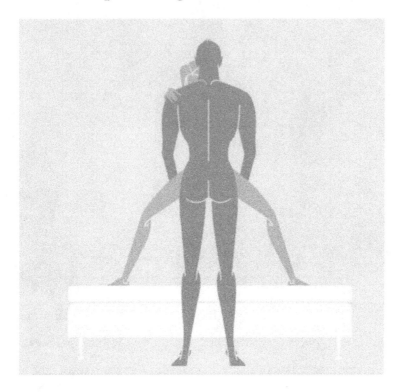

He will stand on the floor in front of her. She will need to adjust her stance so that he can easily slide until their pelvises meet. He'll do all the moving on this one, but she can do whatever she wants with her hands.

Tips: This can be tricky if there is a large height difference.

175. Life Raft

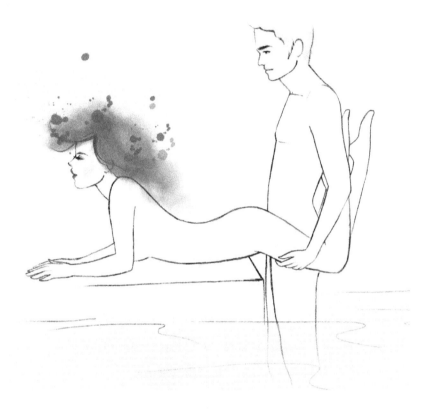

She will position herself on the pool bed on her stomach. Her vagina should be in the middle of the bed. He stands behind her with her legs wrapped around his hips. He should not push downwards. He enters and starts thrusting.

Tips: This is designed for sex in the water. You will need a pool and an inflatable pool bed. The important thing is to make sure the vagina stays out of the water because the water, especially chlorinated, can dry things out.

176. Arched Bull

Another amazing and delightful sex position belonging to the family of sitting and bull sex variations is known as arched bull. It's quite similar to the standard bull sex position, but allows the woman to relax, being outstretched on the ground. This position involves the man sitting on the floor with legs straighten and spread and sustains his body a little leaned backward by placing his hands behind her back on the floor. On the other hand, the woman lays down and sustains her body on elbows between his legs together with their genitals tightly meeting together. The woman places her legs on his shoulders with slightly bent and close her feet behind his neck to keep him close to her body. This position gives free hand to the woman as she can move according to her will, allowing her to make miracles with her body, and the male partner can just be watching and admiring it. Being laying down on the floor, her body is fully exposed to her male partner, who can feel delighted and mild by seeing her beautiful cuts and shapes. He can caress her breasts if she's leaned a bit forward and getting hands free from supporting his body. Sight-seeing would be too amazing, sensational and fantastic as the penis goes deep inside the vagina and rubs her inner lips to make room for his inclusion. This also allows a huge clitoral stimulation, which will provide countless orgasms. Try to opt for it to give your partner a surprising delight.

177. Open Bull 180

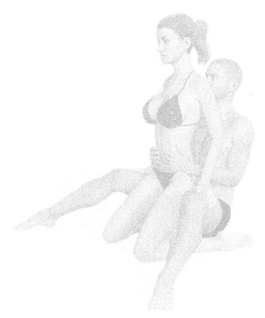

A profound sitting position belonging to the bull variation is open bull 180. This position seems quite amazing while looking at its demo. This involves the man sitting on the ground with his hands on the floor to sustain his body while his legs are half-folded and lifted from the ground, driven apart to make room for his lady. While the woman sits on his lap that is half of the actual area due to the folding of the legs. She sits and leans forward a bit to allow front and back entrance to the penis. As she sits on the penis, therefore, the bending of the penis miscalculates its inclusion. This position delights the man with intense kissing and licking experiences as both partners are too close to each other. He can kiss and lick on her neck, shoulders, head, and face and back to delight her for sexual intercourse. This position also allows breast access with hands to put forward and caress her breasts. The woman feels a bit uncomfortable in movement as she has less room to move around and feel the penis going in and out. But rocking and tilting the ass together with changing the angles could make it a fiesta for both of the partners.

Tips: Try to opt for frequent sex if you are at the advanced level of sex. Your partner will definitely love it.

178. Planted Arched Cowgirl

It involves the man, lying on the ground with the upper body lifted, which sustains himself with fists on the floor. While the woman, being on top, sits on his abdomen, arched backward just like in the arched cowgirl position. This position allows the man to not only explore the sight-seeing of penis inclusion but also delights him with clitoral playing and stimulates her nerves to go wild towards the sexual approach.

Tips: The woman can open her legs wide apart to give him full access, together with deeper penetration and frictionless inclusion. Woman, being on top, is captivated with controls over penetration and movements according to her choice. The movements mostly come from her side when she lifts, rocks and rotates her hips.

Benefits: Both partners, in this position, can catch each other's emotions and move in a rhythm that will bring more satisfaction for both of them.

179. Big Dipper

He will position himself so that he isn't quite sitting in the chair, with his hands resting on the chair and his feet on the bed or sofa. He will be completely elevated off the ground. He will look like he is going to do a tricep dip. She will then straddle him as she is facing him, but she should not place any weight on him. He will then lower himself and push back up, moving in and out of her.

Tips: This is a tiring sex position, so don't plan on being here too long. You will need a sturdy chair that faces your sofa or bed.

180. Turtle Sex Position

He starts by kneeling in the bed, his butt resting on his ankles. She will straddle him, squatting so he can enter. Both will wrap their arms around one another. This will require a grinding motion and not thrusting.

Tips: This can be a difficult position. It requires some strength and balance for both people.

181. Screw Sex Position

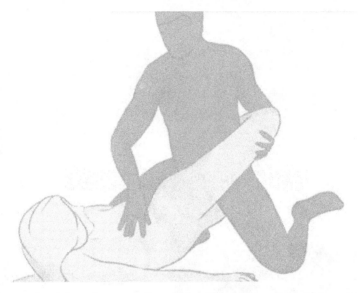

She will start by lying down on her side. He will position himself behind her legs and place his hands on either side of her torso. She will turn her upper body to face him as he starts penetrating her.

Benefits: This is a simple position that anybody can do.

182. Downward Sex Position

She will lie on her back close to the edge of the sofa or bed and raise her legs into the air so that they are pointed towards the ceiling. He will stand in front of her and grab her legs, pulling her towards him so he can enter her. Once he has her lifted towards him, he will lift her waist off the bed so that only her shoulders and upper back are touching the bed.

Benefits: There is a lot of stimulation for both people with this move.

Chapter 17.   Experimental   Sex

Positions

183. The Rocking Chair

Stand astride your man, so that you are face to face. Once it's inside you, wrap your legs around his buttocks and make him do the same. Then you and your man should join your elbows under each other's knees and lift them up to the level of the chest. Then start rocking with forward-backward movements.

184. The Wheelbarrow

In this position the woman stands before the man, who takes her ankles. The woman folds her legs, bringing her knees close to her chest, and leans her legs against his. The man then penetrates her from behind.

Tips: The woman have to keep her balance, supporting her weight. Lift the face often, otherwise the blood will go to head and would risk feeling faint.

Benefits: It allows couples to have sex by stimulating new parts of the body and therefore to experience new sensations, to awaken the senses by putting them into play differently. The senses will hit of life by performing this position.

185. The Drawbridge

The man must form a bridge with the body, while the woman leans against him and let herself be penetrated. Pubis versus pubis, it's a great position if you prefer the rotational movements of the pelvis rather than the classic up and down.

Tips: This position can only be performed if your partner is strong and trained and has no back problems. It is also a position that requires a lot of balance, as your partner has to support your weight and at the same time to rotate the pelvis. He may also try to raise and lower the pelvis, but movement will be limited by your body.

Benefits: This is a very pleasant position as the penetration is deep and the contact between your pubis is very exciting for the clitoris!

186. The Wheelbarrow 1

The woman is resting on her arms and on one knee. The man is on his knees, holding his partner by the pelvis and her unbent leg leans on his side. It is he who rhythms the movement.

Tips: This position cannot be maintained throughout the whole intercourse because it would be too tiring for the woman.

Benefits: This position offers a great access for G-spot.

187. The Monkey

The man lies down and collects his legs in the chest. The woman sits on him and lets her partner put her feet on her back.

Tips: For more intense stimulation and to help balance, the partners can support each other by holding their wrists.

Benefits: This position is ideal for those who love deep penetration.

188. The Boat

The man kneels at the edge of the bed and penetrates his partner lying on his back. Holding her by the ankles, she slightly raises her legs apart and moves rhythmically.

Tips: Depending on the stature of the man, it may be necessary to use a cushion to lift the partner's buttocks.

Benefits: The penetration is very deep, relaxing for her and particularly exciting for him, which dominates the situation from above.

189. The Indian Headstand

The woman is resting on her hands, her arms are stretched out. The man is at the edge of the bed and lifts her pelvis, while she rests her legs on the partner's arms.

Tips: It is a position that requires great agility, a little strength and that cannot last more than a few minutes.

Benefits: It strengthen the muscles of both partners.

190. The Triumph Arc

The man has to sit on bed with his legs stretched out in front. The woman has to get her knees above him, lowering herself on erected penis. Once comfortable, arch the back. Place the head between the man's legs and then grab the ankles.

Tips: The woman should be careful not to strain her back when arching.

Benefits: the man can bend forward and has full access to do anything to your chest kiss you and others.

191. Propeller

The man is lying on top of the woman as in a classic missionary position. While above the woman, maintaining the position gives the momentum to make a 360-degree rotation.

Tips: The woman must guide him with her body, like the propeller over a helicopter, making sure to lift his legs when they swing overhead.

Benefits:
Benefits
This can be tricky to get right and can take practice to master.

192. The X

This position is all about control: your man is lying on his back on the bed. Turn around then straddle above him, so that your back is towards him. Lower yourself unto his erect penis. Extend her legs back towards her shoulders and bring your torso towards the bed, between her legs. With both your legs and your man's legs you will form an X. Then start sliding up and down. To get more thrust use his feet.

Benefits

This will create a great sensation as you will get extra stimulation from his body rubbing on your clitoris.

193. The Head Game

start this game by placing yourself face down, face down. With your hands hold on to the lower back and raise your legs and back, so that it is as perpendicular as possible. At this point your man kneels in front of you, grabs your ankles and puts his knees at the height of your shoulders. Then grab his hands and ask him to hold you by the hips. You will both be stronger. Hold her thigh to leverage and get her genitals to enjoy an otherworldly experience.

194. Gravity

The woman is lying on her back and brings her knees to her chest. He is kneeling in front of the woman, holding his feet. With just the movement of the hips, the man can penetrate her while controlling the movement and helps to keep her in balance. To increase the pleasure, she can put her feet on his chest, holding her hips still further giving him extra control and letting him penetrate even more.

195. Pinball

The woman is lying on her stomach. The man is kneeling in front of her, grabs her pelvis and keeps him at the height of the penis. This position leads to excitement very quickly. For a more comfortable variant, the man is seated on his heels, he draws the partner's pelvis to himself, stroking her clitoris.

196. The Clamp

This position is decidedly complex and requires good musculature for both, particularly for the woman's arms. The woman starts by lying on her side, rising with her left arm and keeping her calves, feet and ankles on the mattress. The man supports her by holding her by the pelvis and, lifting her right leg, penetrates her. Despite being very difficult to perform, it is a position that promises deep penetration and explosive orgasm.

197. Alternating Legs

The woman is lying on her back and puts one leg on the partner's shoulder. He is on his knees and penetrates her holding the ankle of her straight leg with one hand and the knee with the other. By taking advantage of the free hands, the woman can caress her breasts or stimulate the sex of her partner. A variant may be to repeat the same movement with the other leg and so on alternating them.

198. The Acrobats

The man is lying on his back with his legs raised and his knees bent and holds the partner resting on his sex by the hips. It is he who moves rhythmically while she caresses the base of the penis, a particularly erogenous zone.

199. Supernova

The Supernova begins with the classic position with the woman on top of the man, standing on the covers. The man must have his head on the side of the bottom of the bed. She crouches on him with her knees bent and feet well placed on the bed as he penetrates her. The woman bends backwards leaning on her arms and moves until orgasm is reached. When the time comes, she throws herself forward towards the man and leaning on her knees, she pushes the man towards the edge of the bed until she protrudes until her shoulders and arms are completely outside the pallet. At this point the woman moves to the starting position until the pleasure for both is achieved.

Benefits

It can be fairly difficult to get the timings right but is good fun to try out and if done properly can give a great simultaneous orgasm.

200. The Y

She lies on the bed belly down making her body protrude, from the pelvis down, beyond the bed, resting her hands on the floor to support the weight. He positions himself above her, his legs between those of her. He penetrates her from behind. The man can also take the woman by the hips and lift her back instead of lying on top of her.

Chapter 18. Kama Sutra Erotic Massage (Tips)

After the tease, give your partner a few seconds to take in the moment. Then, you can begin with the massage. Again, it is important that you observe his/her reactions, listen to the cues he/she is giving you. These cues will help you determine whether to apply more pressure or less against his/her body.

Do not be nervous about massaging your partner's back. As long as you avoid the spinal area, everything is safe. Start with light strokes. If you feel that he/she likes it a little harder, you can apply pressure as necessary. Do the massage with long fluid strokes.

1. Neck and Shoulders

Pour oil on your hands and rub your palms together. Keep your hands moist and warm. Begin by stroking your lover's neck and shoulders. Massage these areas in continuous circular motion starting from the neck and moving slowly toward the shoulders. From the shoulders, work outward to his/her arms. Apply firm but broad strokes. Massage the areas for the next 10 to 15 minutes.

2. Side of the Spine

Pressure should not be applied directly to the spine. Tackle the side of the spine instead. You can begin from left to right or right to left. It does not matter as long as you meticulously care for both sides.

Stroke the side of his/her spine in a continuous movement. From massaging his/her shoulders, continue the movement to the side of the spine and down to his/her hips.

Use your fingertips for light stroking and the heels of your palms to add more pressure as necessary. Add more oil if needed. This will help make your strokes smoother and more fluid. Keep working on his/her back for the next 10 minutes. Take your time. Do not rush the movements.

3.   Back of the Legs

Do not apply a kneading technique in any part of your partner's body. Remember, tantric massage is about slow, long and firm strokes. When working on his/her legs, you should apply gentle pressure only. It will be a good idea to stroke his/her legs once again with a rough and soft textured item. Pick his/her favorites. Continue stroking his/her legs gently and slowly.

Work your way down until you reach his/her feet. Circular and continuous stroking is essential in this area. Massage each foot one by one. It is best to use your thumb for the stroking. Massage your lover's legs and feet for the next 15 minutes. Focus more on the legs as you can work further on his/her feet once he/she is turned over.

4.   Turn him/her over.

After mindfully touching your lover's back, rest your left hand on his/her tailbone. Your right hand should be placed at the back of your partner's head.

Breathe in deeply through your nose and breathe out slowly through the mouth. Keep your hands steady as you continue to breathe deeply. Take a few minutes before you gently ask the receiver to turn over and lie on his/her back.

5.   Restoring balance in the Chakras

Once your partner is lying on his/her back, make sure he/she is comfortable. Provide a rolled-up towel to support the neck and back of the knees. Now you can begin with incorporating the balancing of the chakras.

6.   Feet

You worked on the feet just a little from the back. Now, you can thoroughly care for it. Using the thumb is ideal in this area but if your lover is ticklish, you can opt for using the palms instead.

This is a sensitive area filled with nerve endings. Your warm touch on his/her foot is enough to give your partner a different kind of sensation. With your fingers and palms stroking it gently and continuously, you can imagine the ecstasy.

Start from the back of his/her toes. Find the fleshy mound. Massage it gently then continue at the back of the foot. Avoid applying too much pressure on the arch. Stick with firm yet gentle touching. Continue stroking from the toes down to the heel. Spend at least 3 minutes on each foot.

7.   Front of the Legs

Like you've tackled the back of the legs, apply firm and long strokes from your lover's ankles to the thighs continuing the stroke from the feet. The thighs and calves need gentle massaging only. Remember that your goal is to provide a pleasurable massage.

8.   Belly

From the front of his/her legs to the thighs, continue stroking him/her meticulously to the hips until you reach the belly. Lay your hands flat and massage this area in circular strokes in a clockwise motion. Avoid applying any pressure in the belly. It is not necessary. Try slow and gentle touching instead with your palms. Your touch should give your partner comfort. Keep caring for this area for the next 3 to 5 minutes.

9.   Chest

Before continuing the massage, rest your right hand over your lover's heart chakra. Take a few minutes here. Breathe in t

After a few minutes, rest both hands on his/her chest. Stroke lightly and apply light pressure. Keep your palms flat as you massage his/her breasts. Gently touch the lymph nodes and apply tender pressure to the nipples.

Try various kinds of strokes and pay attention to what he/she likes best. Continue with the chest massage for 10 minutes.

10.   Head and Shoulders

From your lover's chest, move your hands to his/her head in a continuous movement. Use your fingers to stroke the scalp. Spend a few minutes in this area before you run your fingers to his/her forehead. With your index and thumb fingers, apply gentle strokes to the area. Do not rush the movements. If you need more oil, apply some on your hands as necessary to keep the strokes smooth and fluid.

From the forehead, move your hands to the side of your partner's face down to the neck and shoulders. Apply the same motion like you did when massaging the back of his/her shoulders - long, broad strokes.

11. Arms

Move your hands slowly from the shoulder to the arm. Again, use firm and long strokes in the area. Work all the way down to the wrist. Spend equal time on each arm. Light kneading in the arms is welcome. Feel free to apply the massage technique in this area.

Continue from the upper arms to the wrist all the way to the fingers. Keep your partner calm, relaxed and connected.

Do not forget to meticulously care for each body part. It is all about mindfully touching your lover's body.

Genital massage is an option that some masseuse may offer. Since you're doing this for your romantic partner, you can feel free to involve the genitals. Again, it is something you should talk about so he/she can know what to expect and relax into the process.

Conclusion

The Kama Sutra is the epitome of an intimate sexual relationship. This book has covered all of the basics, especially about how the Kama Sutra is about more than just sex. It is about the connection with your partner on an emotional and spiritual level. This book is written to teach a novice about how to set the mood, and how to hold your partner, with a few positions to try out.

The Kama Sutra is about loving your partner and showing them by exploring every inch of their body. It is not about being considered a "sex god," but about being an attentive lover.

Remember, sex is an incredibly important part of romantic relationships. There are a ton of health benefits related to having sex regularly, including improved immunity, increased heart health, lower blood pressure, pain relief, decreased stress and improved sleep, better libido, and so much more. After reading this book, I hope you were able to gain a fantastic understanding of past and current sexual activities along with a variety of different ways to spice up your own sex life and enjoy yourself and your lover on a more intimate and sensual level. Sex can be as intimate or as shallow as you make it; however, meaningful and passionate sex is almost always preferred. With this book, you should be able to understand the initial purpose of the Kama Sutra and the principles that surrounded it.

One of the most significant issues in today's relationships is that people aren't exploring each other's bodies the way they used to. With this book, I hope you can enter the bedroom with confidence to please your loved one and the willingness to do whatever it takes; and I hope they feel the same way. The Kama Sutra was right when it spoke of finding someone compatible with you anatomically and attitude-wise. Someone who has a high sex drive isn't going to mesh well with someone who has a low sex drive. You may be able to make it work on an emotional level, but on a physical and sexual level, your relationship may fall short.

Granted, sex isn't everything in a relationship, but it means more to some people in a relationship than it does to others, so choose your lover wisely. This book should have also shown you different ways in which women may have seen you in the past and the future; the same goes for women and how men view them. In modern times, we don't care much about the way people see us, but in ancient times, your reputation was everything. This book can be an eye-opener to how some of your current behaviors may have been seen in ancient times – whether that affects you or not is your own accord.

Aside from many asinine doings involved in recipes, spells, and charms, there was also a lot of educational and exciting information on aphrodisiac foods and which ones work the best. Some people might not even realize the large number of foods that can be arousing to specific individuals. We all have the things that arouse us – scribble that in on the aphrodisiac section.

It is very easy to slip into a life of routine, which isn't necessarily a bad thing unless it has to do with your sex life and learning. Two things you should never stop doing: learning and experimenting in the bedroom. Take the knowledge you have received from this book as either a grain of salt or as your new sexual bible. I hope you enjoyed it!

The connection of the bodies should not end with orgasm but should continue long after both are replete. A man and woman should come together in mind, body, and spirit. Such is the essence of the Kama Sutra; such is the Art of Love.

Thanks for reading this book.
If you enjoyed the content, please leave a good review, it will be useful to me. Thanks in advance!

CPSIA information can be obtained
at www.ICGtesting.com
Printed in the USA
BVHW072203220221
600780BV00005B/290